MW00780721

Hearing and Doing

Hearing and Doing

The Speeches in Acts and the Essence of Christianity

Christopher R. J. Holmes

BAYLOR UNIVERSITY PRESS

© 2022 by Baylor University Press
Waco, Texas 76798

Unless otherwise stated, Scripture quotations are from the New Revised Standard Version Bible, copyright 1989, Division of Christian Education of the National Council of the Churches of Christ in the United States of America. Used by permission. All rights reserved.

Cover and interior design by Kasey McBeath
Cover image: Giovanni Paolo Panini, *Ruins with Saint Paul Preaching*, ca. 1735, oil on canvas, housed in the Royal Collection of the Museo del Prado

The Library of Congress has cataloged this book under ISBN 978-1-4813-1786-3.

Library of Congress Control Number: 2022938611

Contents

Introduction

There is nothing more generative of theology than Holy Scripture lovingly received in faith. Scripture determines theology's themes, call, and vocation. This book represents something of a listening exercise. What follows is an instance of scriptural theology. The focus of this study is the speeches in the Acts of the Apostles. Acts is, as Augustine says of Scripture in general, "a text lowly to the beginner but, on further reading, of mountainous difficulty and enveloped in mysteries."[1] Acts is accessible to infants in the faith and confounding to experts, should there be such a thing. This is because Acts, as Calvin writes, contains "the whole substance of the faith."[2] I think that is true, and so have written a book that communicates something of the substance of the faith in a way that is informed by the speeches in Acts.

What exactly is "the whole substance of the faith"? We will see that it has to do with God and how all things may be said to relate to God. We come to know and love the faith of the Christian church, and learn to endure in what it confesses with respect to God, from the narrative of Acts in general but the speeches in particular. The speeches are profoundly instructive and moving of the appetites and affections in relation to God. Indeed, we must,

Calvin notes, "have hearts harder than iron if we are not moved by the reading of this narrative."[3] The speeches are a feast, not just doctrinally, though that is certainly true, but also in terms of the lessons in moral perseverance they provide. There is an overabundance of spiritual food in the eighteen speeches in Acts, and so one must be selective. But how?

The approach pursued here is a thematic one via the main speeches of Peter and Paul.[4] Calvin speaks of six points therein: "the mercy of God, the grace of Christ, the hope of blessed immortality, the invocation of God, repentance and the fear of God, and other principal points of heavenly teaching."[5] If that is a felicitous description of the "sum total" of Christian confession, then is there also an overarching theme that the substance unfolds?[6] Yes, I think that there is. The theme of Acts is the kingdom of Christ, its "pattern (*ratio*) and nature . . . and what sort of state and condition it had in the beginning."[7] The principal points of divine teaching that Peter's and Paul's speeches contain, united as they are by the grand subject of the "kingdom of Christ," are the book's focus. More specifically, I pursue the book's great theocentricity. Acts' focus is God. It is important to consider these six points representing "the sum total" in relation to God. God, his being and attributes, makes all the difference for understanding divine mercy, Christ's grace, blessed immorality, and so forth.

Instead of either having fifteen speeches and therewith fifteen chapters, or focusing on the eight speeches of Peter and the seven of Paul's, Peter's speeches are first canvassed in this work so as to elucidate their profound underlying theocentrism, the vertical dimension if you will. Peter's speeches, centered as they are around Jerusalem, concern the first half of the narrative of Acts, while the second half of Acts is about Paul's doings. Acts is about God, first and foremost, "the mercy of God." Acts is also about the Son of God, the "grace of Christ." Acts also concerns the Holy Spirit, which takes us into the domain of "the hope of blessed immortality." Peter's speeches are, accordingly, mined for their instruction regarding the metaphysics of the message of God: the mercy of the Father, the grace of the Son, and the hope of the Spirit.[8] I ask: What does Peter teach us and assume to be true about God via the gospel of the kingdom as he proclaims it? The focus of the first three chapters of the book is Godward, the objective heart of the kingdom.

The focus of the latter three chapters is Paul's speeches. I consider their import for what Calvin calls the "actual fellowship of the godly."[9] The consideration is then on us in relation to God, the moral dimension if you will of the message that Paul proclaims to Jews and increasingly the Gentiles throughout Asia minor. I offer an account of Paul's speeches with a view to their imperative dimensions, that is, what they would have us do. Paul's speeches encourage "the unflagging endurance of the servants of God under a huge burden of troubles."[10] This is not to suggest for a moment that we leave God behind as we consider the import of Paul's speeches for our later three themes, namely the invocation of God, repentance and the fear of God, or other principal points of heavenly teaching. Instead, we shall see how these points relate quite specifically to an important divine person and agent in the narrative, the Holy Spirit of God.

My main goal in writing this book is to encourage hearing and doing. What do Peter's speeches help us to *hear* with respect to God, and what do Paul's speeches help us to *do* in relation to God? The aim is to draw attention to the speeches themselves in order that these mysteries of which the speeches speak might become dearer to us. I also have a secondary goal in mind in writing this book, and that is to speak to contemporary conversations regarding the doctrine of God. I engage, from time to time in part 1 of the book, dimensions of the first two volumes of Katherine Sonderegger's magisterial work, *Systematic Theology*. In her first volume, she treats the attributes of God, and in her second volume the Trinity.[11] Sonderegger is a fitting dialogue partner because she writes of God in a deeply devotional and biblically charged manner. That said, I am concerned that her "metaphysical compatibilism," as she calls it, is inadequate for describing the relationship of God to what he creates and upholds in being.[12] To argue as she does that God's nature is his relation to the world is not an entirely fitting way to unfold the God/world relationship.[13] The motif of participation has, I think, greater biblical density, theological utility, and promise than "metaphysical compatibilism."[14] Acts helps us to see why. Moreover, the relationship of God to the world has to honor the priority of God the Father not only in terms of the triune life but also in terms of what the Son and Spirit accomplish in mission in relation to us. While there is a great deal of material to commend in her writing on God, dialogue with Sonderegger's work sharpens our reading of the speeches and their prioritizing of God (the Father), thereby correcting certain dimensions of her account of the relation between the uncreated God and created things. Again, I think teaching on participation, rightly understood, has more biblical traction than does metaphysical compatibilism.

Another conversation to which I contribute in parts 1 and 2 is the place of Christology in describing the relation of God to creatures. Rowan Williams, in his remarkable book *Christ the Heart of Creation*, conceives of "incarnational revelation" as the key.[15] While there is something to that, I am not convinced that Williams' account of Christ quite aligns with Jesus' own God-directedness and the theocentrism of Acts. There is a need to consider afresh Jesus Christ as the way to God, as one who is from God and of God. Jesus' actions and voice are, it goes without saying, transparent to those of God. Dialogue with Williams' account clarifies what is at stake, theologically speaking, in terms of appreciating Acts' description of Jesus as one who is acted upon by God (the Father). That the apostles proclaim something as happening to Jesus—namely, God raising him up—reforms our sense of Jesus' mission and what it means to speak of him as the heart of creation. Jesus Christ does, as Williams maintains, "generate a new and fuller grasp of the 'grammar' of createdness."[16] My rejoinder is that Jesus' own God-directedness—his theocentricity—generates a distinct description of creatureliness understood along more participatory lines than Williams envisages. Just so, Sonderegger and Williams will feature as dialogue partners in part 1. Their judgments receive both encouragement and also some modification in relation to Peter's focus on God, the concomitant sense of Jesus as one acted upon, and Peter's encouragement of a more participatory account of creatureliness.

Further to this, in terms of the moral dimension and part 2 of the book, I bring into relief the foundation of the imperatival dimensions of Paul's preaching, namely "divine authority." Moral authority relates, as Oliver O'Donovan argues, principally to God as one who self-discloses "in creation and providence."[17] I explore in part 2 how God's authority relates to creation and providence understood along more participatory lines. How does the created order's moral structure receive authority by virtue of its participation in God? What shape does God's authority have, morally speaking, when he creates and sustains things as participations in himself? We receive help in these matters from Paul's own form of life. Paul commends his own form of life as worth imitating because it participates in and corresponds to God, the God who is the context for Paul's actions and their intelligibility. I ask, what are we to learn from such commendation? Paul's acts have the kind of God-relatedness that they do because they not only refer Godward but also enjoy a kind of participation in God. In part 2, I unfold the rationale for Paul's apostolic commendation of his own form of life.

If Scripture received in faith is the most generative source for theology, what nonscriptural voices from the great tradition will inform our reading? Beyond living voices such as those of Sonderegger and Williams, who will sharpen and receive some correction from our engagement with Acts, who from the great cloud of witnesses will tutor us in terms of receiving the substance of the faith as Acts communicates it? The reader will encounter, first, the Genevan reformer and humanist John Calvin. Calvin is a master exegete. His commentary on the text is clean and unencumbered, written with a view to the instruction and edification of the faithful.[18] I do not always concur with Calvin's conclusions, but he is the first port of exegetical call. Calvin is both Reformed and catholic, something that I strive toward. He is reformed insofar as theology is always subject to ongoing reformation by the self-authenticating and perspicuous word of God; catholic insofar as he recognizes that theological formulations ought to inhabit and promote the conciliar tradition, a tradition that is, in the words of the twentieth-century Anglican theologian E. L. Mascall, "a perpetual source of new and exciting discoveries."[19]

A premodern exegete, theologian, and pastor such as Calvin is also an ideal exegetical conversation partner because he is not inhibited by the constraints of the modern tradition of biblical commentary. There is of course a place for careful technical work in relation to the text, but the technical side of things is of little interest or concern to me.[20] I do not have the skills, aptitude, or disposition to do such work. I am after the plain sense of the narrative (and the speeches therein) in its indicative (metaphysical) and imperative (moral) dimensions. The speeches have things to show us if we would but open our hearts and minds to them. If we are to receive them, we must be spiritual (or on our way to becoming spiritual) people. The plain sense of Scripture I embrace assumes that Scripture, as an instrument by which God sanctifies us, has things to teach us. Scripture encourages us, moreover, to imitate God as the means to receiving those sanctifying truths. Furthermore, with respect to Calvin, I think that he is an ideal interlocutor because, as Hans Boersma insightfully states, "no theologian has tied the vision of God so closely to a divine pedagogical program as Calvin."[21] I attend in this book to Peter's vision of God and how his proclamation of the gospel takes up space, horizontally speaking, in the moral, political, appetitive, and affective counsel Paul provides to the fledging churches to which he speaks in his missionary journeys. Calvin is my listening mentor in this regard.

That said, I am also very interested in the theology of St. Thomas Aquinas. Thomas will be the main systematic interlocutor—for he never wrote a commentary on Acts—but only insofar as what he writes helps us hear the speeches and do what they commend to the end that God be glorified. I make frequent reference to Thomas, sometimes over and against Calvin. However, my goal throughout is to help the reader indwell the speeches and contemplate the themes present therein with Calvin as our exegetical tutor and Thomas as systematic interlocutor, illuminating as it were the God/world relationship presented in Acts. You could think of this book as a short one-volume systematic presentation of the faith, alert to both the many strengths and the occasional weaknesses of the twenty-first century's most important work on God, Sonderegger's *Systematic Theology*, and its most perceptive work on Christology, Williams' *Christ the Heart of Creation*. To the extent that Thomas is serviceable to that goal, I draw upon him. This will generate not only a better understanding of Acts and its message but also, and most importantly, the "sum total of Christianity."[22] In short, this book is a serious contribution to systematic theology. It is a contribution to neither technical biblical scholarship nor international Calvin (or Thomas) research. It is a listening exercise involving a discussion with theologians, the primary one being from the sixteenth century, the secondary one being from the thirteenth century.[23] This listening exercise is also an intervention, an encouragement to think about the God/world relationship along more participatory lines. Let us turn, then, to the speeches with a view to considering their import with respect to God (part 1) and us in relation to God (part 2).

Part I

Peter and the Metaphysical Dimension

1

The Mercy of God

Mercy and the Expulsion of Defects

We begin with mercy, the deep care of God evidenced toward sinners. Mercy does something, and that is it expels defects. In this chapter, we consider God's mercy and the work it undertakes among us, contemplating mercy's salience as divine mercy.

Peter's first speech in Acts 1:16–22 begins, not surprisingly, with Scripture. Peter cites Scripture in order to locate Judas' apostasy. The preaching of the apostles originates in Acts with the witness of Old Testament Scripture as to what must be fulfilled. Why? Because the words of Scripture are those of the Holy Spirit. The words of David in the Psalms are those of the Spirit who foretells, through David's words, Judas' actions. The agent of foretelling is the Spirit, and as we attend to the Spirit's prophetic speech, we see what God does with Israel's chief defect, unbelief.[1]

The first divine person we hear about in the speeches is thus "the Holy Spirit" (Acts 1:16). The ministry of the Spirit is described as one of foretelling, and what the Spirit foretells is the action of an apostate culminating in his suicide. If we are to begin to receive the mercy of God, we must begin here, that is, with the betrayal of Jesus on the part of one of his own. Judas' betrayal, however, is Israel-like. Judas simply does what his own people did throughout their disastrous history. Israel repeatedly betrays its Lord and, in so doing, encourages the nations to do the same. Judas is truly "a guide for those who arrested Jesus" (1:16); likewise, Israel's disobedience encourages Gentile hostility to Jesus.

The judgment that the Spirit foretells regarding Judas' apostasy, which assumes Israel's apostasy, is, however—and thankfully—not the last word. This is because of God. Thus we ask: Where does God fit into this? We must look at what happens to Jesus, who was crucified but even then was "taken up from us" (Acts 1:22). Jesus is not only raised from the dead but also "lifted up" as it were by God (1:9). The God we encounter in the opening chapter of Acts is present in this act, the lifting or taking up of Jesus to heaven. Mercy's form, its effect, has something to do with Jesus, and what God does with him is take him up. Herein, most surprisingly, God begins to heal our defects via the resurrection of this man.

Why does God not restore the kingdom to his people? Why the taking up of Jesus when it is the clear expectation of the disciples that the kingdom be restored? The taking up of Jesus is the means by which the gospel is established. The gospel's aim, Calvin writes, is that "God should reign in us."[2] That God would achieve his reign in us by taking Jesus up to heaven is extraordinary and also counterintuitive: consider, for example, that God lifts Jesus up, and that God promises the indwelling Spirit even though the Spirit has always been active foretelling (though not indwelling). As we noted a moment ago, Judas' apostasy, his apostasy being the last gasp of Israel's apostasy, is also foretold. But more than that, if we are to think about mercy, here, it has to do with God doing something rather surprising: taking Jesus up. In so doing, God creates the time to draw near to God's perfect kingdom, what Calvin calls "participation in the glory of God."[3] The end of Jesus' being taken up is participation in God's glory (Acts 1:22). This is true of us too: participation in the divine glory is what the mercy of God ultimately achieves for us through the lifting up of Jesus to heaven.

Peter's opening speech leads the hearer toward divine mercy. Mercy has the form of overcoming what was long ago foretold through, astonishingly, God taking Jesus up to heaven. Apostolic preaching is anchored in Jesus, who is no longer corporeally present. Accordingly, we begin to see that what Calvin calls a "kind of vast treasure" is before us in Acts. God's mercy, the mercy of the Father, has a transformative character. God transforms the pride that lies at the heart of Judas' abdication, which itself reflects Israel's abdication and encourages Gentile abdication, "into a means of blessing."[4] And yet, mercy is also a rather hidden affair, for God lifts up Jesus, taking him out of our sight in such a way that he is no longer corporeally present.

Thomas helps us to see what is at stake. Divine mercy in its scriptural fulfillment "is especially to be attributed to God." Mercy is of God. It is proper to him. Mercy dispels "misery, whatever be the defect we call misery."[5] Judas' defection, repeating as it does Israel's, and guiding as it does the Gentiles, is dispelled by mercy. Mercy dispels "wickedness" (1:18). That is mercy's effect.[6] Mercy, moreover, has a source, and that is God's goodness. "Mercy," John Webster explains, "is the directing of God's majestic goodness to the relief of the creatures in misery and wretchedness."[7] Mercy is, ultimately, what Thomas calls an "aspect of goodness." God's goodness is inherently communicative, and what it communicates to creatures is perfection. So Thomas: "It pertains, therefore, to the nature of the will to communicate as far as possible to others the good possessed; and especially does this pertain to the divine will, from which all perfection is derived in some kind of likeness."[8] Thomas notes that the good God perfects things. Divine goodness thereby expels defects. Such giving is proper to mercy; for mercy dispels misery. Mercy perfects us in relation to the Father, the giver, as James states, of "every perfect gift" (Jas 1:17).

In Acts 2:14–36 (after the giving of the Spirit), we hear a second and far lengthier speech of Peter's. Calvin comments that Pentecost "reflects the marvellous goodness of God, in that a punishment for human pride was transformed into a means of blessing" for all.[9] Divine goodness bestows perfection, thereby dispelling misery, the misery of unbelief as foretold by the Spirit. Nevertheless, mercy's restorative character does not appear in the expected form. Instead of God restoring "the kingdom to Israel," God lifts up Jesus (Acts 1:6), and God's lifting up of Jesus is the means by which the blessing of Pentecost arrives.

The theocentrism of the book of Acts is already making itself apparent. We cannot make sense of Judas' apostasy without the Holy Spirit's foretelling, and we cannot make sense of Jesus' ascension to heaven without God, who lifts him up. "He was lifted up" (Acts 1:9). What does this say about divine mercy? Is mercy most appropriately said of one person or of the whole undivided Trinity? More specifically, how is mercy related to Christ's being "nowhere visible in the world?"[10] The effect of Christ's being lifted up is that the most extraordinary gift, the gift of the Spirit, is given. The "promise of the Father" poured out at Pentecost remedies, repairs, and indeed restores the church over and against its betrayal (Acts 1:4). Divine mercy dispels gloom, invoking instead "prophecy" (2:18); stupor is overturned in favor of prophecy, misunderstanding toward understanding, all because of "the promise of the Father" (1:4). Acts is, as we are beginning to see, about God at work dispelling misery, whether it be in the form of individual or corporate apostasy.

The Definite Plan

The revelation of divine mercy is anything but domesticated.[11] The Old Testament prophet Joel's fiery language, cited by Peter in Acts 2:17–21, is associated with profound ills. Not only does Joel anticipate Judas' suicide, but Joel's prophecy's fulfillment is also manifest in the sun's turning "to darkness" and "the moon to blood" (2:26). The most terrible thing is that the "man attested to you by God" suffered the ultimate ill, crucifixion, and death (2:22). Is this too a revelation of divine mercy? If so, what is, in fact, God's role in Jesus' death? And how does this impact our nascent account of mercy? Jesus, attested as he is by God, was "handed over to you according to the definite plan and foreknowledge of God" (2:23). We see here in Peter's second speech a theme that we saw in his first speech in chapter 1 associated with Judas' apostasy. On the one hand, the handing over is our doing. God "lays no necessity upon His creatures."[12] Creatures are free to defect, and defect they do, though their defection is not necessary. And yet, on the other hand, Peter's speech clearly teaches that God ordains Christ's death. Jesus' death is "according to . . . [a] definite plan" (Acts 2:23). God's plan is manifest in Christ's death, which is not for a moment to deny that creatures exercised their free will in putting Christ to death. Thomas writes of this mystery that the creature's "being moved by another [God] does not prevent it being moved from within itself."[13] We must not simply oppose God's will and acts to those of creatures.

We find here two discrete agents at work. God moves Jesus to the cross, and Israel hands Jesus over, freely. There is no competition between the two, though they are not exact coordinates.[14] God foreknows the Israelites handing over, though such foreknowledge is not the condition of this tragic event. To speak of Jesus' crucifixion apart from God's "definite plan and foreknowledge" is as problematic as attributing it simply to the human agents involved (Acts 2:23). Equally problematic, is the notion that divine foreknowledge is causal. Let me explain, carefully. Jesus dies according to God's plan; he is "killed by the hands of those outside the law," persons who actively will his death (2:23). Describing the crucifixion on both levels as, on the one hand, according to God's plan insofar as God permits it and, on the other hand, evidence of our verdict upon him points to how God works in a noncompetitive way. Each way of describing Jesus' death as according to God's permissive will in conjunction with our actively rebellious will has integrity of its own. As David Fergusson writes, "God and creatures do not compete on the same causal plane."[15] God's foreknowledge is not causal, though God wills some things to take place contingently. Instead, God foreknows it according to God's plan and promise. The event cannot be abstracted from either.

God's plan is inclusive of Jesus' crucifixion and our collusion in it. This is mercy's shape.

The mercy of God is illuminated as well by the words "see and hear" (Acts 2:33). Peter speaks these words by reference to the Spirit. One might expect the word "hear," for many have heard the believers speaking "in their language, as the Spirit gave them ability" (Acts 2:4). What is surprising is that the Holy Spirit is seen. How is the Spirit, an incorporeal person, seen? The Spirit is seen in the divided tongues "speaking about God's deeds of power" (2:11). Those deeds of power are manifest in what God has done, namely, make Jesus "both Lord and Messiah" (2:36). Herein, we see the mercy of God on display in the Spirit seen declaring God's deed of power. Those deeds show, as Thomas notes, God "doing something more than justice." God's mercy does not eliminate justice but "in a sense is the fulness thereof."[16] In mercy unfathomable, God not only raises Jesus but makes him "Lord and Messiah" (2:36). God honors his promise to put "one of his [David's] descendants on his [David's] throne" by exalting the murdered Jesus to his "right hand" (2:33). What Peter presses is elucidated by Thomas' sense that mercy, as the fullness of justice, does not result in "sorrow." God does not respond to the verdict "of those outside the law" by being "sorrowful at heart" (2:23).[17] No, God is not, Thomas continues, "affected with sorrow" by the profound antipathy that is demonstrated toward him and the misery that inevitably follows. Instead, God does something that we can see. The Holy Spirit, as seen and heard, lets "the entire house of Israel know with certainty that God has made him both Lord and Messiah" (2:36). Mercy is neither mute nor invisible. Mercy acts (visibly) so as to dispel misery. The Holy Spirit is seen and heard in the deeds of God manifest in the raising of Jesus. God does not 'belong' to our defection. Instead, God dispels it in a way both seen and heard. This is mercy.

God's mercy is true. On the one hand, we are, as Calvin says, "like lazy donkeys." The "threats and intimidation" characteristic of Joel's vision are the means that God uses to stir us to "seek salvation."[18] On the other hand, "lazy donkeys" that we (Gentiles) may be and complicit as we are in Israel's handing over, we, says Peter, nonetheless know whom we gave up: "as you yourselves know" (Acts 2:22). Thankfully, it does not belong to God to act as we do. There is not any disjunction in God between what God knows and does, whereas what we know—that this man (Jesus) is attested by God—does not lead us to act in ways commensurate with what we know. Our knowledge is not coextensive with us as is the case with God. As Ulrich Zwingli writes, "The Deity is simple. Hence nothing can be done by Him to which all His attributes do not equally contribute."[19]

Put in a different register, God is not passionate. God does not act under compulsion but responds freely. This too is mercy.[20] God cannot act in a way incommensurate with what God knows. God's heart is always pure, acting as he knows; hence God commends purity in human beings. Calvin notes, "But whoever has a pure heart perceives God with the purity of inward vision as often as He shows Himself."[21] So the call Peter issues is to purity, for only then do we perceive the mercy of God at work in the crucifixion of Jesus. Indeed, we come to know that God witnesses to this man, "Jesus of Nazareth" (Acts 2:22). However, without clean hearts, we will not act on that knowledge by repenting and being baptized. Instead, we will remain enslaved to our passions, thinking that God is more like one of us. Thankfully, Peter reminds us that God is not one of us. What God knows—goodness—is what God does: God communicates goodness for God is goodness, absolute and uncreated goodness itself. So Thomas: mercy, "absolutely considered, pertains to goodness," for the good God bestows "perfections on things," namely the purity of heart that acts in a way congruent with the revelation of Jesus the Messiah.[22]

Mercy and Power

The attribute of God that we repeatedly encounter in Peter's speeches is power. "Why do you stare at us, as though by our own power or piety we had made him walk?" (Acts 3:12). The preaching of the gospel of the kingdom takes place with power. Power is of course what the believers receive when "the promise of the Father"—the Spirit—is poured out (1:4). The healing in 3:1–10 that precedes Peter's third speech in 3:12–26 evokes an appreciation of God's power—and not so much mercy, though the miracle is a clear response to human need.[23] If power is the divine name that is perhaps the most prominent in the opening chapters of Acts, why draw attention to mercy as I am doing? Thomas illumines our thinking in this, noting "God's omnipotence is particularly shown in sharing and having mercy."[24] God can and does do what is beyond the capacity of created nature; indeed, "God can do all things that are possible absolutely."[25] The power of God, as with the mercy in which it is especially shown, directs us to what is above us. After all, the "man lame from birth" enters the temple, "walking and leaping and praising God," God who delights in doing infinitely more than we can ask or imagine (Acts 3:9). Power's effect is the "participation of an infinite good," the great goodness of God that encounters us as mercy, dispelling misery.[26] The healing of the lame man reflects his new relationship with God, his participation in a fresh way in the infinite good that is God. This means that the power of God, whether manifest in relation to Pentecost or the first miraculous healing recorded in Acts 3:1–10, is never detached from the divine goodness. God's goodness is comprehensive of his power, and his power is shown in his mercy, which in turn effects a more intense participation in the divine goodness than was had previously.

The healing episode also reminds us that God is not powerful in relation to some other thing. Even more, God's power is not the "principle" of the healing.[27] The principle is, instead, even more basic, God's essence. This is a subtle but important point. God acts through his essence. God does not act as God does because of something outside himself; God is not acted upon in any kind of determinative sense by what is not God. God's goodness is one with his essence, for God is essentially good. God is not made good. Accordingly, God does things that are impossible for created natures whose goodness is had in relation to God. We see that in God's making the lame man jump. The formerly lame man's praise of God heralds something of the goodness of God as exceeding "created things beyond all proportion."[28] The end or purpose of this healing is the man's good, and this goodness—his walking and leaping—is unintelligible apart from the divine good, God as one who is essentially good. God governs and directs things in accordance with the good he is. And God's goodness is not limited to what is possible for creatures. Herein lies its power, and power is shown in "having mercy."[29]

The God-centered response of the man is also quite instructive. Peter and John give him "the name of Jesus Christ of Nazareth," and what the man gives forth is praise to God (Acts 3:7). This contradicts the response of the people "in Solomon's Portico," the "Israelites," for they direct their response toward humans, namely Peter and John (3:11, 12). The Israelites look to "particular goods" as opposed to the "universal" good, God himself.[30] The healing, understood as a particular good, has a reference, and that reference is God. Though "the name of Jesus Christ of Nazareth" effects the healing, praise is directed not to him but to God (3:7). The relentless Godward thrust of the text is clear. It is God who receives praise, just as it is God who "glorified his servant Jesus" by lifting him up (3:13).

The Israelites whom Peter addresses assume a horizontal horizon for the healing. They recognize that it is good that the man is healed, but they fail to see that "the end of the government of the world is the essential good."[31] The end of the healing is, in other words, God. The man's healing is exemplary because he responds to his healing not as the Israelites do—attributing it to Peter and John—but to God. In this respect, the man becomes more Godlike rather than less in his "walking and leaping and praising," thereby moving "others to be good" (Acts 3:8).[32] We see this dynamic at work in Acts 4:4. Many of those who heard Peter's sermon in 4:8–12 become better: they believe. Mercy, as anchored in goodness, perfects. A defect is removed, that being unbelief. "The priests, the captain of the temple, and the Sadducees" persist in defecting, but Peter's preaching comes with power (4:1), and belief is the perfection that Peter's preaching encourages. This too is mercy. The perfection given—belief—generates a more God-like form of life. It also makes us more creaturely. Belief expels unbelief, and unbelief is expressed by the leadership's annoyance at Peter's preaching. It belongs to God's mercy to expel what prevents us from being assimilated to God.[33] Expressed in an explicitly Thomistic idiom, God does not let Peter's address return void. God gives the things he creates and preserves, "this perfection," namely belief.[34] Peter's address, which is of God, receives its perfection in the belief of "about five thousand" (Acts 4:4). It would not befit God to address us as he does without blessing us with the faith to receive him. "The faith that is through Jesus has given him this perfect health in the presence of all of you" (3:16).

In addition, it is worth considering why the theodicy question (why was this man born "lame from birth"?) is never asked (Acts 3:2). Does not the man's condition belie what Thomas teaches regarding creation as inclusive of preservation? Why indeed are there defects in the first place? Furthermore, are defects not God-caused if everything that the creature has is received? In an extraordinary statement, Thomas writes that "God cannot cause a thing to tend to not-being, but a creature has this tendency of itself, since it is produced from nothing."[35] Defects, expelled as they are by the perfection given to things by God, are not God-caused. God does not cause the man's lameness just as God does not cause the annoyance of the priests, the captains, and the Sadducees. Again, God does not cause defects—"*you* handed over and rejected Jesus" (3:13). Now, we must be careful here. The man's lameness is not because of sin. Jesus forbids us thinking that (cf. John 9:1–12). But the man's existence, his being as it were, is precarious because he is dependent on alms. Without alms, he would likely die of hunger. An intermediate cause—alms—sustains him in being in relationship to being itself. God (again) cannot cause defects; also, God cannot cause sin. But God does cause creatures who are "produced from nothing."[36] However, what is from nothing moves to nothing.

The lame man is not defective because he is lame. He has a defect, and that is his being from nothing, which is true of all of us. The defect is that he, as with the rest of us, cannot be without participating in God's goodness. The language of defect is not a moral one. Rather, it is a comment on his (and our) creatureliness. The leaders' annoyance with Peter and John is, however, a defection that is sinful. They have agency, in other words, free will, and they choose, freely, to will wrongly and thus to defect, absconding thereby from mercy. God's mercy meets the lame man, reversing the tendency of all created things to revert to nonbeing. The man receives "perfect health" and, as with those Peter calls "friends," great "times of refreshing" (Acts 3:16, 17, 20).

The mercy of God is such that it bestows on things perfections radically disproportionate to their being: the man becomes God-like, his perfect health anticipating his sharing, eternally, in the life of God, who is life itself. Why then does God not incline the will of the leaders by "an interior inclination" in such a way that they too receive "times of refreshing" (Acts 3:20)?[37] Why do they tend toward nonbeing by rejecting their Messiah? Strictly speaking, we cannot answer this question. This is because their rejection has no exemplar, no reality in God; rejection has no ontological basis. Unbelief, and more basically sin, does not preexist in God. Accordingly, we may only tend toward what is of God as there is "nothing wholly evil in the world."[38] Thus our defection has to do with our corrupting the good. God does not author sin—we do; we damage the gifts given to us. It is solely due to God's goodness, his "liberality," that there is anything at all.[39] The lame man's existence as with the existence of those around him is indicative of divine liberality. Divine mercy is the "conferring of good above that which is due"; divine judgment is the conferring of what rejection entails.[40]

Foreknowledge

No one deserves the gift of existence (a work of nature) let alone the forgiveness of sins (a work of grace). Both are gratuitous. It is only appropriate, then, to think with Peter about God's foreknowledge and how it relates to God's mercy. Accordingly, I consider why that which is created good destroys itself so wantonly and willfully. Acts 3:18 is indeed the second instance in which we encounter, the first being Acts 1:16, the language of "foretelling." As concerns the latter instance, the Holy Spirit foretold through David of Judas' apostasy; as concerns the former, God foretold through the prophets the Messiah's suffering. Here, as elsewhere, we are in delicate theological terrain. Some might argue that either the Spirit's or God's foretelling of either apostasy or suffering implies foreknowledge: one only foretells what one foreknows. The matter at hand is, however, a bit different: it has to do with the relationship of foreknowledge to the divine will. Foreknowledge is not equivalent to will. God's knowledge has to do with God. God knows what God is, and God is love. Therefore, God cannot know what is not of himself, as is clearly the case with Judah's apostasy and the Messiah's suffering. Similarly, because God is merciful, as we have been noting, via the healing of the blind man, God cannot *know* the Messiah's suffering in the same sense that God knows himself. Judas defects, and the Messiah suffers Judas' and his people's defection. If in knowing himself God knows all things, then our description of Israel's apostasy and the Messiah's suffering—which is itself caused by Israel's leadership's apostasy in conjunction with Gentile guidance—is intelligible only on a different level and with a different register than divine knowledge. Thus it is fitting to deploy the language of foreknowledge.

Just so, we must not conflate God's knowledge of himself with God's foreknowledge. God, in knowing himself, knows all things, and God, in willing himself, wills all things. This is clear. And this is the basis upon which there is a difference between what God knows and what God foreknows. God does not will his people's apostasy just as God does not will in any immediate sense the Messiah's suffering. Instead, as Calvin reminds us in his *Institutes*, God's "decree" has to do with God's "concern for the whole human race, but especially his vigilance in ruling the church."[41] That is helpful because God's will is never detached from God's mercy, his concern for humanity, revealed in his dispelling of misery in Jesus Christ. What Peter's speech teaches us is that foreknowledge pertains to sin; foreknowledge pertains to what is not of God, that is, sin. Judas' apostasy is of course sinful as is the disobedience of Israel that culminates in its Messiah's suffering. While God does not know sin, God does foreknow it, and, in fact, God permits it. This much we must say. What circumscribes foreknowledge is "concern" or, better, mercy.[42] More than this we cannot say. God foreknows evil but does not will it, for God can only know and will what is commensurate with himself.

Think for a moment about what Peter says of the Israelites' rejection: "friends, I know that you acted in ignorance, as did your rulers" (Acts 3:17). There is genuine agency expressed in Israel's rejection of its Messiah, rejection that God foreknew according to his plan of "universal restoration" (Acts 3:21). Israel's handing over was not accidental. And yet, Peter's surprisingly concilia-tory remark is instructive. Sin in whatever form is enveloped by mercy. God foreknows that we will act ignorantly. Even more, that ignorance—which reflects malicious intent on our parts—is only known as such in relation to divine mercy: "He whose property is always to have mercy."[43] Put technically, the epistemic principle of apostasy is mercy. The God who foreknows our apostasy and the suffering of the Messiah in responding to it foreknows and foretells in accord with his mercy. God foretells not sin but sin suffered, vanquished, forgiven, and, ultimately, repelled.

Here, I respectfully depart from Calvin. Whereas for Calvin providence is "the determinative principle for all human plans and works," I think it is better to say that it is God's providence, full stop, that is God's knowledge of his "definite plan" for the flourishing of his creatures. This knowledge is coextensive and convertible with God himself, for whatever truly is in God is God. God acts by his actuality; God's providence is his essence. Accordingly, it is not false to say as Calvin does that providence's principle is "God's will," but it is inadequate. An account of God's will must be housed in an account of God's attributes, the goodness and love God is, God's essence in short. Israel's apostasy is foreseen by God, though this does not mean that it is willed by God. What is willed by God is instead the good, the promise of God: "The Lord your God will raise up for you from your own people a prophet like me" (Acts 3:22). The cause of Israel's salvation is God's will revealed in the promise, and what God wills is never in contradiction to God. Foreknowledge refers only to what disagrees with God's will—disobedience. In sum, God does not will "ignorance," but God does foresee "ignorance." God is never said to be ignorance's cause.

The Priority of the Father

Let us step back from a technical but vital conversation encouraged by Peter's speeches so far, asking, what may we be said to glean from Peter's speeches with respect to God and God's mercy? We are already receiving, I think, a strong sense of God and of God's grandeur. What makes the apostles speak as they do, keep "speaking about what we have seen and heard," is God (Acts 4:20). Calvin comments, "For what is the whole world compared with God."[44] To stand in awe of God, this we must do, and in order to encourage us and attract us to God by what Calvin calls "the delightfulness of His grace," God effects miracles.[45] Similarly, "it is no small comfort to know that God is with us," even in the midst of spiritual disasters.[46] We also receive herein a strong sense of God's mercy. The gospel has to do with God doing something, effecting something, namely, his kingdom. And what does God do? The theocentric character of the message is clear. God raises Jesus; God exalts him; God gives repentance and forgiveness; and God gives the Holy Spirit, who "witnesses" together with the apostles "to these things" (5:32). The narrative of Acts, while commonly thought to first and foremost be about the Spirit, is rather more about God. God the Father's priority and primacy in Peter's speeches, as is the case with the eternal Godhead, is emphasized. The acts of the three persons of the Godhead express their respective relations of origin, that is, paternity, filiation, procession, and spiration. Jesus is raised and exalted because he is from the Father; the Holy Spirit is given because the Spirit proceeds from God the Father through the Son. The mission of the Son and Spirit reflect their origins with respect to the Father.

What is extraordinary is, moreover, that God the Father's priority in terms of order in the blessed Trinity does not displace Jesus and the Holy Spirit. Jesus leads and saves, and he does so because God raised and exalted him, and the Holy Spirit "witnesses to these things" as "given" (Acts 5:22). Likewise, there is no competition among the persons. They work as one because they are one. And what they are is mercy, with the Father as mercy's fount. Consider Calvin's comments on 5:31: "Repentance is indeed a voluntary conversion, but what is the source of this willingness except that God changes our heart." We repent—no one else can do that for us. That anyone repents is because of God (the Father). The God who raises and exalts Jesus and who gives the Spirit "changes our heart," and he does so through Jesus Christ and the Spirit.[47] This is mercy in all its triune fullness revealed with the Father as the fount.

Said differently, the Father's priority is seen in another way in Acts 5:31: "God exalted him at his right hand as Leader and Savior that he might give repentance to Israel and forgiveness of sins." Christ saves, and it is through Christ that sins are forgiven. But Christ reconciles us not to himself but to God. Those who are being reconciled are, furthermore, "fashioned again in newness of life by the Spirit of regeneration."[48] The life in which the Spirit fashions us is the life common to the Father, Son, and Spirit, the life that is coextensive with their one single essence, the life that the Son and Spirit eternally receive from the Father, being begotten and proceeding. The "Gospel has its foundation in God," and what we say of God (the Father) is not only his priority and precedence in the life of the Trinity but his presence in mercy in overturning our hanging of his Son "on a tree" (Acts 5:30).[49] God changes hearts, "converts reproaches," all because he is good and in his goodness effects mercy, dispelling unbelief. As Robert Jenson insightfully notes, Israel's history is narrated not "as a 'history of salvation' but rather as a story of uninterrupted spiritual disaster."[50] That disaster culminates in Jesus' hanging. But what does God do with that? God raises and exalts him, granting repentance and forgiveness, blessing him with the Spirit, the same Spirit poured out among us. This, too, is mercy.

Considering the mercy of God along more systematic lines, mercy is revealed in what Jaroslav Pelikan calls, in his excellent *Commentary on Acts*, the text's "dual emphasis."[51] For example, Israel is guilty of hanging the Messiah on a tree even as this act was foretold. Though I think, as mentioned previously, it is appropriate to say that God permits the Son to suffer and that his sufferings are foreknown, we must not overemphasize this. To do so would be to distort the "dual emphasis" that the speeches honor; it would also compromise our attentiveness to the essence of God's mercy. As Augustine reminds us, God is "deeply hidden and yet most intimately present."[52] This is true even with respect to Israel's leadership championing, with the help of surrounding Gentiles, Jesus' crucifixion. The plans of the wicked do not upset those of God. After all, God desires, following Paul's extraordinary argument in Romans 9–11, to "be merciful to all" (Rom 11:32). God is "intimately present" to his people inasmuch as he is accomplishing something through them—their salvation—without excusing them. What God foresaw—their apostasy—is subject to himself, all that he is. God's mercy is inclusive of Jesus' death, for his killing is never abstracted from his being raised. God in profound mercy accomplishes salvation via ignorance amounting to the Messiah's killing. And as Thomas reminds us, the principle of all of God's acts "is [ultimately] the divine essence itself."[53] In his essence, God is supremely good, and, in his great goodness, God perfects our ignorance by using it to bring about our forgiveness. This is mercy and is reflective of the "dual emphasis."[54] Mercy, too, is one and simple in God in that it is the principle of the expulsion of the main creaturely defect, sin, and its twin, unbelief. So God's essence is the principle of all God does. The effects of God have their source in the attributes of God, which are coextensive with

God himself. The effect we are considering—the raising of the one crucified through ignorance—is because of God, and this effect belongs to his mercy. Divine mercy does not condone apostasy, but it does contextualize apostasy in such a way that it shows apostasy to be as foolish as it truly is.

What ultimately generates the conciliatory tone of Peter's speeches, especially his speech in Acts 3:17–26, is God. Commenting on Acts 10:34–43, specifically verse 35, perhaps in what is Peter's subtlest speech, Calvin says that "God recognizes in every single man His own work, one should rather say, Himself."[55] What is the principle for such recognition, especially in light of the "dual emphasis," that Peter is keen to preserve? It is God's goodness. And how is that goodness experienced, via mercy, on those (which is all of us) who directly or indirectly killed his Son? Does God still recognize himself in us? God is in what he has made insofar as what God creates participates in a relationship of likeness to himself; God thus recognizes himself in his work. God's work, by varying degrees of likeness, continues to be upheld by his presence to and in it; God upholds what he causes, for God is, after all, a preserving and perfecting cause. There is no such thing as a person or people entirely devoid of God's likeness. Accordingly, we may say that God is present in ignorance, while not excusing it, present in the form of mercy. No one is entirely devoid of participation via likeness in what is proper to the one essence of God himself, even in the case of a people who hand his Son over to death. Jesus' crucifixion is not the last word.

Devoid of Likeness?

Let us pursue this line of thought as we consider the gift of the Spirit to the Gentiles, the remarkable effect of God's command for the apostles to preach to the people that Jesus "is the one ordained by God as judge of the living and the dead." "Lord" and "judge" is who Jesus is: he bears the divine name and executes a work proper to God, "judge of the living and the dead" (Acts 10:42). Indeed, "God shows no partiality" (10:34). This is good news. Peter argues that the reason that God shows no partiality in relationship to either Jews or Gentiles is that God needs neither in order to be God. As Calvin reminds us, God's "existence is in Himself," and God is the one "in whom all things subsist."[56] Everyone in every nation has their existence in relationship to God. The acceptable response to that reality is that of fearing him and of doing what is right. To fear God is to recognize that one does not subsist in relationship to oneself. When we do right, we testify, moreover, that there is another to whom "right" refers. The category of "right," surely a moral one, has an underlying metaphysical designation, and that is God. We exist, yes, and we do so as participants via likeness to God.

Our existence is a participatory one. We subsist in God, as Calvin notes, but more than that we participate in God. Our existence is in God. The reverse is of course never true: God's existence is not participatory. God just is. This assumes what Katherine Sonderegger describes as "the metaphysical compatibility of creature to Creator."[57] What subsists in God is also compatible with God. But there is more than that. For Sonderegger, God communicates his being to creatures and is humbly present "in all existents."[58] There is nothing wrong with describing the God/creature relationship this way. But it is inadequate as there is too strong an emphasis on God's self-communication. This is in part the Barthian imprint on her thought. What is lacking is a strong sense of created things as participations. Creaturely being is participatory being. Just so, God does not so much indwell things, as Sonderegger avers, but rather creates things that refer to God by virtue of their participatory character. The creature/Creator distinction—the ever-greater dissimilarity between Creator and creature—is better honored, I think, by conceiving of created things as enjoying a participatory relationship with their Creator. Being is "bestowed," yes, but the being bestowed is participatory being.[59] The creature's relationship is, properly speaking, a participatory one. With this in mind, we avoid the notion of "admixing" that Sonderegger champions.[60] Such a note compromises the very aseity of God that she—rightly!—wants to safeguard as well as the dissimilarity (which is always greater than the similarity) between God and creatures.

In terms of Cornelius' testimony, I think the motif of participation also carries more explanatory weight than does Sonderegger's metaphysical compatibilism. That Cornelius prays faithfully and fervently as he does—see Acts 10:30–33—gives us a glimpse of (Gentile) creaturely subsistence in God. It is natural for creatures who subsist in God to pray to God, though of course many do not. Cornelius acknowledges before Peter, the believers from Joppa, and his household that he stands in God's presence. God's presence is what they are "in" (10:33). Participatory thinking has greater power than does "metaphysical compatibilism" to explain the crucial preposition "in." The listeners are not simply present to God, though that is true. Even more, they are "*in* the presence of God" (10:33). Sonderegger emphasizes how "the Intelligible lives *in* the concrete."[61] Cornelius, however, places more weight on how his—and all those gathered—ability to listen assumes their being in God's presence. Cornelius is in God's presence. This indicates more than an "echo [of] the Sovereign Life of Almighty God."[62] What is intimated by Cornelius is a general or common participation in God's presence. However much we may abscond from it, we cannot undo what we are, creaturely participants in the unparticipated God. And it is this God who structures our being in such a way that God-fearing persons cannot but reflect on themselves as existing in his presence.

The relation of Jews and Gentiles to God is clarified by patient reflection upon God's presence. God is present to all. God accepts all those who fear him as the one before and in whom they exist. Rowan Williams' learned treatment in *Christ the Heart of Creation* treats Christ as revelatory of what "the analogical relation of finite and infinite actually looks like." Likewise, I think that an understanding of creaturely existence as fundamentally participatory in nature is elucidated by the notion of analogy—"no similarity," as Williams notes, "without an always greater difference."[63]

Where I differ with Williams is in terms of the theological work Williams assigns to Christology in unfolding analogy. Christ proclaims and reveals the kingdom, thereby directing us Godward. The doctrine of creation establishes the difference between Creator and creature: we exist in God's presence, as Calvin recognizes, and not the reverse. Jesus Christ, the Spirit-anointed one, does good and heals, but he does so in relation to God, the one who anoints and who is with him (cf. Acts 10:30). The Son's "liberating dependence" on the Father "that is the filial relation in the divine life" grounds, for Williams, "created dependence on the Creator."[64] That said, the heart of the doctrine of analogy is, I would argue, not so much what is said of Christ as revelatory of a relationship but what is simply said of God. The one God shows no partiality because all those to whom God is present—which is all of us—exist in him. What is said of God "substance-wise," to use an Augustinian idiom, grounds creatures. Christ the judge, the Lord of all, directs creatures Godward in such a way that they participate ever more deeply in what is said of God "substance-wise," including existence itself.

Mercy and Prayer

This brings us to the realm of mercy, too, for "God hears" Cornelius' prayers (cf. Acts 10:31). God "thinks him [Cornelius] worthy of the light of the Gospel."[65] As with all people everywhere, following Paul's argument in Ephesians 2:3, Cornelius is a child of wrath "by nature." The nature Paul speaks of is one contaminated by sin, contamination that of course God judges; God's wrath is but his love burning hot over and against our sin, thereby destroying it. At the same time, our nature is not "destitute of all grace."[66] Cornelius is evidence of that; for Cornelius responds to God's presence. Even then, however, the ultimate cause for God loving Cornelius as God does is God himself. Calvin writes, "God finds the cause for loving us in Himself alone, and that He is moved by His own mercy and not by our merits."[67] This too is mercy. As John Webster notes, "Creaturely need is the occasion of God's mercy, but not its cause; its cause is simply the incomparable, ceaseless goodness of God."[68] There is nothing in us that would make God love us; our needs do not cause God to be beneficent. Why then does the angel appear to Cornelius, showing God's favor as the angel does? Because God is merciful. God, furthermore, accepts those who fear him—whether Jew or Gentile—as the one in whom they subsist. The goodness and kindness of God draw persons to himself, whether they be Jews or Gentiles.

Remarkably, we encounter God's goodness and kindness in an altogether unexpected way. It is seen through a message that God sends and that God preaches, and this is the message God sends and preaches "by Jesus Christ" (Acts 10:36). We could never hear God in all God's grandeur without aids and helps. God, accordingly, addresses us in an accommodated way. Jesus Christ is the form that suits our ability to understand, "for God was with him" (10:30). We need this form because, as Calvin notes, "how many deign to listen to God specifically?"[69] God knows that we, or most of us anyhow, would rather not listen to him. We are hardly attentive to the works of nature declaring the glory of their Creator. But there are always a few who are "upright and God-fearing," as was Cornelius (10:22). Peter's preaching instructs this upright man and indeed all those in his household in God's way. After all, Peter knows that faith "does not exist without teaching," and the teaching Cornelius receives is that Jesus "is Lord of all," that is, "the one ordained by God as judge of the living and the dead" (10:36, 42).[70]

How does this relate to mercy? First, none of this is by necessity.[71] What Calvin calls "the holy silence of faith" recognizes that whenever we have to do with God we are on the receiving end.[72] We remain likenesses, images as it were. God nonetheless gives "the gift of the Holy Spirit" even to the Gentiles, those thought to be least worthy of his attention (Acts 10:45). It is proper to divine mercy to remedy defects, in this case, that Gentile hearers of the word may also receive the Holy Spirit—"even to the Gentiles" (10:45). God, in his great goodness, expels this defect that has accompanied Peter's preaching thus far. Until now, Peter's preaching lacks the desired fruit, Gentile tongues and voices that extol God. Without the inclusion of uncircumcised believers, Peter's speaking is still defective. In mercy as deep as it is wide, God uses a Gentile—Cornelius—to remedy the defect present in Peter's preaching thus far. Even though "all the prophets testify about him that everyone who believes in him receives forgiveness of sins through his name," it is not until now "that everyone" is understood to include Gentiles (10:43). The gospel is good news for everyone. The mercy of God, abundantly present in this speech, is, once again, at work, expelling the defect of Gentile unbelief, and, once again, the goodness of God, communicating perfection, evokes faith, Gentile faith. Gentile believers are perfected by the Spirit falling upon them. Their faith, hitherto lacking the Spirit and thus defective, is perfected. This also is mercy.

Mercy and Law

The last matter we handle, briefly, in this chapter is law. In our antinomian cultural moment, we resist law, thinking it antithetical to mercy. What we discover in Peter's speeches, however, is a profound sense of law as an expression of mercy, indeed mercy's excessive character. We now look to Peter's final speech in Acts 15:7–11, again considering its theocentricity and what light it sheds upon the divine mercy via the law. As with Peter's previous speech, this speech presents God as the active agent. In the last speech of Peter's, God shows, accepts, sends, preaches, anoints, raises, allows, and ordains. This God does. And as we have seen in our exploration of mercy thus far, mercy involves God "doing something more than justice." God's justice assumes his mercy, and his mercy, as an expression of his goodness, encounters us "more bountifully than is proportionate to their [our] deserts."[73] The "brothers" who Peter addresses in his eighth speech (Acts 15:7–11) are recipients of God's goodness. God's goodness is perfective, helping them, through the Spirit, to see that there is no longer any "distinction between them [Gentiles] and us [Jews]"

(Acts 15:9). This is mercy. If God's goodness were proportionate, then it may well still be the case that the law—the "yoke"—that the "ancestors" have been unable to bear would still be with them (Acts 15:10). As Thomas notes, "God's justice and mercy appear both in the conversion of the Jews and of the Gentiles." "In cleansing their hearts by faith," God effects Gentile conversion through the gift of the Spirit (Acts 15:9). It is God's justice, avers Thomas, that is seen inasmuch as God acts according to "the promise made to their fathers."[74] However, there were no promises made to the Gentiles. The Gentiles' conversion, indeed, their salvation, is "more than justice."[75] God has a debt to himself to fulfill when it comes to Israel's salvation—the promise made to the ancestors. But when it comes to the salvation of the Gentiles, we are in the territory of excessive goodness, a goodness that is the fundamental principle of God's action in saving Jews and Gentiles "through the grace of the Lord Jesus" (Acts 15:11). This, too, is mercy. Even though no promises were made to the Gentiles, God nonetheless reconciles them too as God's promise includes the blessing of the nations, overcoming their defects as well as Israel's.

Put differently, God orders Israel to himself according to his law. The law's purpose, in its ceremonial and moral dimensions, is to order Israel to God. This is why it is a gift: gifts bind us to the giver. And yet, this gift, when placed "on the neck of the disciples," is called a "yoke" (Acts 15:10). How can a gift be unbearable? Is it then no longer a gift? Let us consider this carefully. The law of Moses is from God. It is God's law, and nothing that God gives or communicates to his people is bad. What makes the law a yoke to Jews is that the righteousness demanded by the law cannot be supplied by the law. There is of course nothing faulty with the law. "What then should we say? That the law is sin? By no means!" as Paul famously writes (Rom 7:7).

There is a parallel available with respect to the knowledge of God nature supplies. Though it is not saving knowledge, it is nonetheless good. The order of nature clearly manifests God, encouraging us to join in its praise of him. Nature is as such good.

The law, too, orders us to God as it is from God. The law is as such good. What we cannot bear is being ordered to God. What is good becomes for us something bad, an unbearable "yoke." It is grace, "the grace of the Lord Jesus," that makes it otherwise (Acts 15:11). As John writes, "For the law was given through Moses; grace and truth came through Jesus Christ" (John 1:17).

Jews and Gentiles "possess," in Calvin's austere words, "nothing but the stuff of death."[76] We cannot renew and remake ourselves, content as we are with death. God "knows the human heart" (15:8). All human hearts are, as Karl Barth notes, "Israelitish."[77] This does not surprise God, and yet God remains merciful, especially in relation to his ancient people. God does not disown them. God wills to be "preeminent" among them as among the Gentiles, establishing in both genuine religion. Here again, we see how theocentric Peter's speeches are. Again: God chooses; God knows the human heart; God testified to the Gentiles; God gives the Spirit to Jews and Gentiles; God cleanses hearts by faith, making no distinction, and it is God whom the Israelites put to the test. Salvation comes from God; it is God's work. Peter, being an excellent "interpreter of God," helps us to see God's preeminence in all this, the God who is preeminent in mercy.[78] As we have been noting all along, God gives to not only Jews but Gentiles the Holy Spirit, perfecting in them the aims of the covenant articulated in Jeremiah 31:31–34. This is of course a surprise, the inclusion of the Gentiles, but what is expelled in them is what is expelled in Israel, namely the greatest defect, unbelief. This is mercy, that God would give the faith that perfects, expelling sin in Jews and Gentiles, cleansing hearts by faith through the gift of the Spirit, thereby fulfilling in the greatest mercy the law's aim.

As we bring this chapter to a close, then, we see what an excellent "interpreter of God" Peter is. His eight sermons instruct us in God, specifically, God's mercy. The sermons teach about the "something more" that God does.[79] The "something more" is seen in the conversion of Gentiles. Not only is God just in fulfilling the promise to his people. God exceeds his justice in absolute mercy by saving Gentiles too "through the grace of the Lord Jesus," not obviating the law but fulfilling it (Acts 15:11). There is much more to learn about the substance of the faith from Peter's speeches. There remains the grace of Christ and the hope of the Spirit. That said, those themes also serve to deepen our understanding of divine mercy and its expulsion of defects. Even then, however, we do not leave the principle of grace and hope far behind, for God remains preeminent. There remains "the grace of the Lord Jesus" through which we are saved, and the principle of that grace, the good news, is God. Grace, as we shall see in the next chapter, precludes the notion that God is indebted to us. This whole chapter has shown how God's mercy reflects God's indebtedness to himself. God fulfills in us what God contains, indeed is, goodness itself. And God does so far "more bountifully than is proportionate" to what we deserve.[80] When it comes to grace, it too has this excessive character, though its register is quite different, for grace is spoken of Jesus Christ. Let us then consider Peter's great speeches from this angle: What instruction do they offer us regarding the grace of Christ?

2

The Grace of Christ

Grace and Witness

Acts' theme is the kingdom of God, and the presupposition and end of the kingdom is, not surprisingly, God.[1] Acts is a relentlessly theocentric book. We continue to unfold the book's theocentrism, but we do so now in a way sensitive to the grace of Christ. Even as we cover new ground so to speak, our sense of God's mercy will be expanded. When we think about the pattern, nature, state, and condition of the kingdom, we indicate Christ and, as I will argue, his grace. Grace is of the Lord Jesus Christ.[2] God is the kingdom's foundation, its center in Jesus Christ. Who heals and restores us to friendship with God? It is the grace of Christ, grace itself as expressive of the fundamental goodness of God. Grace is, I will argue, the love of God effecting new goodness in things. Accordingly, our soul is, by God's grace, elevated so as "to a participation of the Divine good."[3] We shall consider in this chapter how the grace of Christ effects that participation in divine goodness. The ground for such consideration is the whole set of Peter's speeches, especially his last speech in Acts 15:7–11, one that paves the way for the Jerusalem council and the transition to the second half of Acts, centered as it is upon the missionary endeavors of Paul. Accordingly, our question in this chapter is simple: What is the

29

contribution of Peter's speeches to our understanding of the grace of the Lord Jesus Christ?

The first thing we need to reflect on is the relative absence of Jesus as an active agent in the Acts of the Apostles. As we saw in the previous chapter, God (the Father) is overwhelmingly active in the narrative. God (the Father) is the preeminent agent. Jesus' agency is more indirect, hidden even, often oblique. Jesus is acted upon: he is, for example, "taken up" by the Father (Acts 1:11, 22). Theophilus is, moreover, told about "all that Jesus did and taught" (1:1). In Peter's speeches, Jesus is, for the most part, not described as an active agent. God and the Holy Spirit are, but Jesus is not. Jesus is, nonetheless, present from heaven as the one to whom witness is given. However, as Calvin insightfully states, "spatial distance does not prevent Christ from being always present with His own."[4] Although Jesus, Peter says, no longer goes "in and among us," he is present (Acts 1:21). But how, and how does his invisible heavenly presence relate to grace?

Peter and the believers bear witness to a spatially distant Christ, a Christ who is nonetheless present (though invisibly) in "astonishing power."[5] How so? The apostles' witness has power because the one to whom they bear witness is alive, witnessing through them. In terms of Peter's Pentecost speech (Acts 2:14–36), Christ's power is coextensive with his life, risen and ascended. The Spirit has not yet been given, and yet there are already about one hundred and twenty believers prior to Pentecost (cf. 1:15). What the believers, together with Peter, do is (again) "witness." To Jesus (and neither God nor the Spirit) is witness offered.[6] We must consider this. No apology is given for Jesus' spatial absence; there is no sense in which the ascension renders him inert. Jesus, after all, is exalted. He is alive, and the response evoked by his being alive is witness. Witness is the foundational category regarding the apostolic relationship to Christ. Apostles are witnesses of the invisible though spiritually present Christ. By witnessing to Jesus, present though spatially absent, the aim of the kingdom, God's achieving his reign in us, is accomplished. God's rule takes form via apostolic witness.

Jesus is alive, present, though "not in the substance (*essentia*) of His flesh."[7] Amazingly, no anxiety about this is sensed as one reads the narrative. The Lord to whom Joseph and Matthias in Acts 1:24–25 pray is Jesus, and in his absence Jesus, in the power of his Spirit, is spread abroad everywhere.[8] This is evidence of grace. But why? Because if Jesus were not taken up, he could not be attested as everywhere present, not locally present but present in a ubiquitous sense. Grace effects, as Thomas notes, "new goodness."[9] Much "new goodness" is brought about because Christ is witnessed "to the end of the earth" (1:8). His ascension comprehends his cross and resurrection, anticipates our eschatological redemption, and manifests his heavenly authority. It is God in his love who takes up Jesus in order that a great good may come about—a good that is the heart of grace. That good is the *news* that Jesus is alive, and the good that accompanies this announcement is witness "to the ends of the earth" (Acts 1:8). Grace is of Jesus, who achieves profound good by commissioning witness to himself.

As we contemplate Peter's speech at Pentecost, it is important to note with Calvin that "God can give us no more excellent gift than the grace of the Spirit, and that indeed all else is worth nothing without this."[10] The Spirit is also associated with grace though, I think, in a secondary sense. What do I mean? In what sense does the grace of the Spirit differ from the grace of Christ? The grace of the Spirit does not so much differ from Christ's grace but is instead, as Calvin notes, "the outcome of the resurrection of Christ."[11] It is grace that Christ is resurrected and ascends; also, it is grace that the Spirit is poured out. New goodness is achieved by the gift of the Spirit poured out, principally God's indwelling of the baptized and, as we shall see, the inclusion of the Gentiles. Christ, who baptizes with the Spirit, gives, in so doing, a remarkable grace. Christ gives us himself in the Spirit. What does this suggest about the metaphysics of Christ's person as the one of whom grace is spoken? To Peter's Pentecost speech we now turn in order to gain some insight, though we do not leave behind our first and most elementary point. Jesus' relative absence in the narrative does not indicate that he is inert. Instead, the Lord Jesus is at work, bringing about a fresh form of grace, namely apostolic witness.

"He Retains His Divinity"

The birth of the man Jesus Christ is central to our understanding of grace, just as is his resurrection and ascension. Grace relates to his person; Peter's speech explains this first principle. Jesus Christ is a man who, "as man, came forth from the seed of David."[12] The man Jesus Christ has ancestors, chief among them David. In his speech, Peter establishes, first, Jesus' humanity via his Davidic ancestry. The key, however, to this man who sits on David's throne is his resurrection, which David of course foresees.[13] The man Jesus does not experience corruption, Calvin says, because "He retains His divinity."[14] This differentiates Jesus from all of David's seed. The man born of one of David's ancestors—Mary—remains God as he always was and will be. This man, though born in and of a certain line, is divine even as he is born of the virgin. Grace is of a person who is human, a man, and coextensive with him. Jesus' grace expresses the divinity that he shares with the Father from all eternity.

Peter's speeches help us articulate why grace in Acts has a christological density—again, "the grace of the Lord Jesus" (Acts 15:11). The rationale has to do with the metaphysics of Christ's person. In 2:22, Peter tells us that God attests himself through Jesus and that God does deeds through him—"that God did through him among you." Grace has a visible form. God the Father acts through the man Jesus. God is praised, moreover, through the works of the man Jesus.[15] The reason God acts through Jesus, does deeds through him and not through himself, has to do with Jesus' generation, Jesus being eternally born of the Father. God acts through the man Jesus because none other is called "the Son of God according to His eternal Being."[16] Jesus' sending is an expression, in time, of his procession, his being born, eternally, of the Father. Jesus does not do what he does—"wonders, and signs"—on his own steam (2:22); rather, his divinity is the ground, and what his divinity, manifested in time, accomplishes is works of grace. Not only does Jesus have his being in relationship to the Father, but his actions are from him too; the Father acts through his eternally begotten Son. Jesus' action in its totality we call grace; it is from above.

Rowan Williams deepens our understanding of the sense in which Christ retains his divinity in his ministry, though his proposals are, as we shall see, not without their difficulties. Christ retains divinity because of his person. Jesus Christ, Williams writes, lives "the divine life in the mode of reception and response."[17] The soul of the man Jesus is "united to the divine hypostasis." Accordingly, there is "no limit to the receptivity" of such a soul.[18] The man Jesus—understood as an embodied soul—receives everything from the divine hypostasis of the Son. And who is this one but the one generated, the Son who receives from the Father the divine nature via generation. Jesus retains his divinity because he never ceases to be united to the processional life of the Son, that self-same Son who enjoys a way of being begun that has no beginning.

Where I think Williams' thought is inadequate is in his claim that "creation's relation to God . . . is grounded in the Son's relation to the Father."[19] The ground of creation's relation to God is God's divinity, specifically, the divine goodness. God's goodness is evident in his ordering of creation to himself. Also necessary is Williams' affirmation, following Thomas, that creatures are spoken in the divine word.[20] It is important to explain creation's relation to God via what is said of God "substance-wise," to deploy once again an insightful Augustinian idiom. Creatures are grounded by their relation to God, who orders all created things to himself. When we speak of divinity, specifically, that Christ retains his divinity even in death, the divinity he retains is what is common to him, the Father and the Son. The "wellspring" of creation (as well as the resurrection), to use Davison's language, is to be sought in the divine unity, to which goodness is intrinsic.[21] The wellspring of creation is all that is said of God "substance-wise," the God who speaks creatures into being through his word.[22] Similarly, Jesus retains his divinity because all that is said of God "substance-wise" is said of his person as God's one and only Son. When we embrace such an understanding, we avoid the language of paradox. Williams' description of the analogical relation of infinite and finite and the infinite as revealed in Christ is, in his way of thinking, paradoxical.[23] Here I think Sonderegger is of help. The reason Christ retains his divinity has to do with the "Processional Life" of God.[24] The divinity of Jesus just is the everlasting act of being generated from the Father, and what he receives as begotten of the Father is all that is said of God "substance-wise." Jesus does not live the divine life in a receptive mode—the heart of Williams' sense of paradox. Instead, Jesus is the processional life of God as one begotten.[25] It is unwise, I think, to ground creation as does Williams in an event so mysterious, unsubstitutable, inexpressible. Better to say that creation's ground is God, what God is, goodness itself, the God who grounds creatures in being through his word thereby ordering them to himself.

However, when we get to the resurrection it is fine to say that the resurrection's ground is in the Son's relationship to the Father. The Son, even in death, never ceases to be generated, one of the two instances "of a simple class, Procession." Indeed, the resurrection of this man who knows no corruption confirms Sonderegger's basic insight that the divine "Nature *proceeds.*" It proceeds as "a single class, Procession, in which we are to discover two instances, the Eternal Begetting, and Spiration."[26] The divine nature proceeds (in the case of Son and Spirit) as that which is supremely good, in need of no thing. I agree with Sonderegger that "the doctrine of the Trinity needs a robust recovery of the Engine of Unity, the Divine Procession."[27] So too the doctrine of the resurrection. The resurrection's principle is Procession in the instance of "Eternal Begetting." The "mode"—Sonderegger's term—"of God's Processional Life is Goodness."[28] We see that goodness in Jesus being raised. It is that same goodness that is creation's ground, its wellspring. The resurrection as the great act of new creation denotes the pure act of God as goodness itself, for we are turned from death to life. The exiles return home.

An important corollary follows. What determines Jesus' "metaphysical status," his presence at the Father's right hand, and his presence in the believing community via his Spirit, is his generation. What determines his ongoing activity, his liveliness and ministry, is his divinity, the divinity that is his as one generated. He is eternally generate, Mary's Son. The one born to die, to suffer his people's corruption, this "man of suffering" enacts "the Divine Procession as It descends to Its End."[29] Sonderegger is most helpful here. She helps us see that his passion and ignominious death are not accidental but expressive of—and not the ground of—the divine life of the Son. Jesus retains his divinity as "the Self-Offering that is God."[30]

Let us think further about this, for in Peter's speeches we gain great insight into Christ's person. Unlike Christ, the Father does not experience a distinction of natures, for the Father never becomes incarnate. Jesus is not the presupposition of the Father's action, though the Father is the principle of Jesus' action. Jesus is from the Father—though the reverse is not true. Peter declares publicly what was hitherto unknown: the man Jesus is "Lord and Messiah" (2:36). Lord is Jesus' name. This is a name inclusive of a title. Lord is also a name common to Father and Spirit. The Lord Jesus is the Messiah, Messiah being a title denoting Jesus' kingship over his people, a title proper to him alone. Jesus is the Messiah according to the flesh, just as he is descended of David according to the flesh. Grace, in Acts, has this fleshly center. We would never say anything of the Father "according to the flesh," but we do say many things of his Son according to the flesh. The procession of Son and Spirit from the Father and the distinction of natures in Jesus Christ is thus foundational to understanding Jesus' grace. The source of Christ's grace is his filial relation to the Father, and what Christ does among us according to the flesh is gracious, for he effects new goodness among us. Grace is coextensive with the humanity of the Son of God, with the flesh of Jesus Christ, who in his one person makes all things new.

In terms of shedding further light on this important terrain, Augustine is helpful. In his magisterial *The Trinity*, he writes that "the reason he [Jesus Christ] does not work of himself is that he does not (so to put it) be of himself." The reason that the Father does things through Jesus—as Peter preaches—is that Jesus is from the Father. Jesus is not, of course, less than the Father but "is from the other [the Father]."[31] So John: "the Son can do nothing on his own, but only what he sees the Father doing" (John 5:19). The Son does not work of himself because he is not from himself. The distinction between the two natures in Christ, as Calvin develops it in his comments on Peter's Pentecost sermon, is, basically, so far as I can tell, but a restatement of Augustine's rule. Augustine's rule is as follows: "There are then some statements of scripture about the Father and the Son which indicate their unity and equality of substance. . . . And there are others which mark the Son as the lesser because of the form of a servant, that is because of the created and changeable human substance he took."[32] Accordingly, when we talk, following Peter, of God doing wonders through Jesus, of God making him "both Lord and Messiah," we consider such statements according to "the form-of-a-servant rule," saying things of Christ "according to the flesh" (Acts 2:36).[33] Grace has this enfleshed character, and God brings about new goodness through the resurrected flesh of Jesus. Again, it is Jesus Christ (and not the Father) who became man. Scriptural statements in Peter's Pentecost speech have a double reference. On the one hand, some statements, following Augustine's lead, refer to Jesus' human nature, his "being less than the Father."[34] On the other hand, others refer to his being "from the Father in his very equality with him."[35] Grace has a foundation, namely, the origin of the Son from the Father, Jesus' consubstantiality with the Father. The Son's action, "his deeds of power, wonders, and signs" (Acts 2:22), expresses the deepest truth regarding his person—"I know him, because I am from him, and he sent me."[36]

The reason we speak of grace with respect to Christ, the Son in "the form-of-a-servant," has, then, to do with his flesh, his humanity. Grace has this touchable, visible character. It is Jesus who is raised up by the Father, Jesus who perfects our creatureliness by pouring out the Holy Spirit, whom he receives from the Father. That happens because he is one with the Father. Our not having the Spirit is a considerable defect, and, thankfully, Jesus remedies that. Mercy, as we saw in the previous chapter, remedies defects. Jesus in his uncorrupted and resurrected flesh receives the Spirit from the Father and imparts that same Spirit unto us, thereby effecting new goodness among us. The Spirit conforms us to God's image, Jesus Christ, and transforms us into the likeness of God, all because God has made Jesus' enemies (and our enemies too, though often we do not know that) into his "footstool" (Acts 2:35). The grace of Christ assimilates us to God, restoring us to God's likeness, crushing all that would prevent us from imitating him in living a life of filial love in dependence upon the Father.

Grace assumes the Son of God's humility, his making himself nothing. Think about the logic of baptism, which Peter commends, along with repentance in Acts 2:30. Peter's hearers cannot be baptized in the name of God the Father but only "in the name of Jesus Christ" (2:38). We cannot be baptized into the Father's immensity, ubiquity, and sheer difference from us. But the Father does assimilate us to himself in a way accommodated to us, and that is through our baptism in his incarnate Son. Without the incarnation, we could not share in what is of God "substance-wise." The Father lives in the baptized through his Son, who pours out the Spirit that is from him upon them. If the Son of God were not among us as a man who makes himself nothing, we could not receive from him. The distinction—the dissimilarity—between divinity and sinful humanity is simply too great. We could not live into the distinction; it would obliterate us. And yet, the grace of the Lord brings us home because Jesus "retains His divinity" as man.[37] As man, he expresses his divinity among us as the one through whom the Father acts.

The Grace of the Servant

In Peter's third speech (Acts 3:12–26), we hear Jesus twice described as God's "servant" (3:13, 26). The language of the servant is important to think about in relationship to grace, for it further underwrites the supposition that grace brings about new goodness and enriches our sense of Christ's person. As the reader will have likely noted, I am not offering a single definition of grace, but rather a way of thinking about grace that is tied to the scriptural testimony. To use a Thomistic register, grace indicates what perfects nature and elevates it in accordance with the essential goodness of God. Grace is supernatural, helping us to do what we cannot do of ourselves, but it has the form of a servant, Jesus Christ. Grace raises us in order that God might be present in us according to likeness. But such an elevation has a form, the form of Christ, who calls us to take up our cross and follow him.[38] Thus grace is "of Christ." Our task is to now consider how the grace of Christ is illuminated when unfolded via the "servant" motif, that is, "his [God's] servant Jesus" (Acts 3:13).

God glorifies Jesus his servant, "the Holy and Righteous One" and "the Author of life" (Acts 3:14, 15). The man Jesus is God's servant who, "due to the hypostatic union, enjoys a created participation in divinity, which is grace."[39] Participation in divinity is not natural to any of us, including the man Jesus. And yet, due to the hypostatic union, unique to him, Jesus Christ gives life, the life that is truly life, which is a participation in divinity that exceeds us. He continually, as a man, receives from above, and the grace he receives he sheds abroad. Jesus gives grace by giving perfect health to the lame man, the first of the miracles attributed to Peter.[40] Nonetheless, Jesus receives the ability to do this from his personal union with the Father. The Father is not Jesus' servant; Jesus is the Father's servant, receiving from him in all he does. The processional life of God has, in Christ, a term in the world's history. This basic truth is the ultimate metaphysical principle of grace. Jesus *receives* from the Father: a strong asymmetry in terms of the Father and Son relationship is present in Acts as it is in the Gospels.

Let me explain. The Father commands his Son, and the Son serves. The man Jesus, God's servant whom God attests, receives, in turn, grace. His divinity is fundamentally receptive or, to use Thomas' language, participatory. This does not mean that Jesus is less than God the Father. We simply indicate that he is man, God's servant because he comes from God. The man Jesus, a prophet like Moses, is however unlike Moses because he is God. His humanity is personally united to divinity. This is true of him and no one else. Jesus Christ always knows and loves God "in the most intimate possible way." Jesus Christ, who blesses us by turning us from our wicked ways, blesses because he, unlike either Moses or ourselves, *always* loves God. Jesus' service to God is an uninterrupted expression of his (filial) love. Jesus' humanity is elevated and "raised above itself" in such a way that Jesus shares in God's life, the life common to Father, Son, and Spirit.[41] He is always acted upon by the God he serves, which, far from diminishing his divinity and equality with the Father, shows us his filial intimacy in relation to the Father. Jesus Christ receives the Father's favor and bestows grace.

To sum up so far, grace is of Jesus Christ, who, as man, remains wholly God. The foundation of Christ's grace is his personal union with the Father. His humanity participates in his divine nature, common to the Trinity. Christ bestows grace out of this abundant enjoyment of grace. His grace effects what is good, mainly in the form of his pouring out the Spirit and healing the lame man. Such goodness is the means by which we share (more) in God's life.

There is further work to be done, however, for we need to reflect upon how the language of the servant does not represent a diminution of the personal union Christ enjoys with the Father. Peter's speeches, in accordance with the whole trajectory of the narrative of Acts, describe (as mentioned) Jesus Christ as one largely acted upon by God. Jesus is (again) "his servant;" the Father is not Jesus' servant. Far from funding a subordinationist Christology, however, the speeches encourage delicate reflection on the mystery of Christ's person and the nature of grace that is of him. The fact that Jesus is raised up implies that the *man* Jesus "is not intrinsically divine."[42] Humanity is not intrinsically divine but instead a created effect of God. God's servant, this man, in being raised, is, however, "made"—as Peter says—Lord. Jesus' humanity is divinized from the moment of conception by the Spirit in Mary's womb. How are we to understand this? This is due to the hypostatic union. The one person of the Son of God receives, as man, grace, "a created participation in divinity."[43] Such a participation is not natural to anyone, including Jesus. His humanity is graced "in relationship to the uncreated grace and person of the Word."[44] We must proceed carefully here too, remembering that grace is what is additional and above—but not contrary to—nature. The man Jesus "is not intrinsically divine."[45] He is man. And yet, the humanity of this man is nonetheless "an instrument of the divinity."[46] His divine nature, proper as it is to his one person, acts through his human nature. Yes, but the man Jesus, though acted upon by God in the resurrection and ascension, never ceases to be self-moved. Jesus always listens to God, as the prophet he is, and speaks what he hears from God because there is no one else whom he would rather hear. Even so, in his earthly ministry, in the midst of always knowing and loving the God he serves without sin, he is acted upon by that same God. Even more, his humanity is an instrument of his divinity, the former being personally united to his one person.

That said, I think that Peter's speech in Acts 3:12–26 does not lend itself very easily to every aspect of Thomas' account of the hypostatic union, a "personal union."[47] I do not think Peter's speeches—or the rest of the New Testament for that matter—encourage me to think, as does Thomas, that Jesus Christ, "as the Word of God, was able to do all things well by calling his divinity into play." Thomas is clear that Jesus' humanity "is a living instrument, with a spiritual soul." That is fine. But the man Jesus, who is the Word of God, does not have an occasional relationship to his divinity. He is divine in all he does because he is always the Father's eternally begotten Son. Thomas would of course agree. Nonetheless, the language of calling divinity into play detracts from the "personal union" that Thomas, rightly, wants to protect. The man Jesus is sinless, forever enjoying "uncreated happiness."[48] The man Jesus as the Word of God eternally knows and loves God—"the same act in which the Father knows and loves himself."[49] To suggest that he calls upon his divinity does not seem quite right. To be sure, Jesus calls upon the Father, but Jesus does not call upon his divinity. Jesus is truly God and man in all he says and does, though, as Augustine points out, some things said of him are more fittingly said of him according to "the form of a servant" rule.[50]

Leader and Savior

How does this one act "in which the Father knows and loves himself," the act of the Father's eternal begetting of the Son, illuminate Peter's description of Christ "as Leader and Savior" (Acts 5:31)? How might we indwell the mystery of Christ's person and grace? Indeed, what is the basis of Jesus' leading and saving? And what do these offices indicate about his person, and how do they express it? What kind of metaphysic do these offices assume? The first thing we say is that Christ leads on the basis of his sight. Jesus sees the Father and therefore leads us to him, who is unseen. Jesus' heavenly leadership reflects him, whom he sees and serves, the Father. During every moment of his life, from conception onward, Christ enjoys "the full possession of God."[51] Even the great cry of dereliction in Mark 15:34 reflects Jesus' confidence in being heard. Jesus leads us to him, whom he sees, and he leads us as one "perfectly subject to the movement of the Holy Spirit."[52] Grace, then, has this pneumatological dimension. In receiving grace, we receive, as did Christ himself, the gracious movement of the Spirit. The Spirit moves us, moreover, to the Father but always through his servant, the Son. Let us consider this.

Peter tells us that Jesus, as Leader and Savior, gives "repentance to Israel and forgiveness of sins" (Acts 5:11). He gives these things as God, and because he is God, but it is we who so desperately need them, and so he became flesh. The Lord Jesus gives as one who sees and who is "perfectly subject to the movement of the Holy Spirit."[53] He gives the benefits of his passion to us as God himself, for his divinity and hypostatic union are the basis for the benefits he communicates to us. However, before he can lead and save, he must receive "as man."[54] And what he receives in his humanity is exaltation: "God exalted him" (5:31). When we think about Jesus receiving exaltation, we think with respect to his humanity, his human nature, united as it is to his one person. Jesus never ceases to exist, on the level of his divine nature, though when we think of his being raised up, the accent is on his humanity, enjoying as it does a created participation in divinity. What the man Jesus bestows upon us in his exalted state is repentance and forgiveness. He gives these gifts as God. These goods flow from his divine person as exalted. These are (again) delicate matters, to be sure, and Peter's speech in 5:29–32 compels patient consideration of them. This one who is killed, raised up, exalted, and witnessed by the Spirit, this one is God. Who is this man? This man is the Son of God, that is who he is, and grace is of him for gifts such as repentance and forgiveness do not come apart from him, to say nothing of the gift of the Spirit.

The Son of God, the Lord Jesus Christ, is, after the incarnation, a composite, in a certain sense anyhow. I do not mean that Jesus is a mixture of divinity and humanity, something that Matthew Wilcoxen seems to suggest with his rather awkward language about the Lord Jesus being "composed of two distinct natures."[55] He is, rather, one person who unites (without confusing) two distinct natures. There is a kind of threefold rule that applies to Christ's person, scripturally speaking. We see this rule at work in Peter's speeches. Some things Scripture indicates refer to the one person, Jesus Christ, the Son of God. For example, "Leader and Savior" is said without reservation of his one person (Acts 5:31). The one person, the Lord Jesus Christ, truly God and truly human, leads and saves. That said, statements like Jesus' being killed "by hanging . . . on a tree" indicate the second rule, for we attribute them to his humanity (5:30). After all, divinity cannot die. Peter speaks of death in reference to Jesus, anticipating as it were Augustine's "form of a servant" rule. Why? Jesus' humanity exists in relationship to his divinity in (again) a "personal union" and never the reverse. His divinity does not exist in relationship to his humanity.[56] In terms of his divinity, Jesus is consubstantial with the Father (and Spirit). His humanity subsists in his one person. It is difficult to account for Jesus' work in this respect unless we make it clear that the man Jesus exists in the Son and is one with the Son because the Son unites him (the man Jesus) to himself. Accordingly, the Son of God is free with respect to the human nature he unites to himself, but his human nature is not free in relationship to the Son. And so, the second rule reminds us that when Peter says Jesus was hung up "on a tree," the emphasis is upon his humanity (5:30).

Furthermore, when we consider Jesus as one who forgives sins, we see an action that points to his divinity. This illuminates a third rule. Jesus has the authority to forgive because he is God (cf. Matt 9:2–8). He is able to destroy sin by applying it "to his own Person."[57] Jesus is always obedient (unlike his ancestors) because he is divine; his divinity grounds and is expressed in his obedience. Accordingly, when Thomas argues that Christ has the charisms (both sanctifying and charismatic grace), he is spot on. Jesus applies our disobedience to his person, erasing it through his obedience, action that expresses his divinity and oneness with the Father. Though Thomas presses the point that Christ's "soul was united to the divinity," I am more inclined to talk in terms of Christ's humanity—as inclusive of his soul—inasmuch as it is Christ's humanity as the soul's home that sanctifies us, giving rise, in the Spirit, to obedience where there was previously only disobedience.[58] Jesus forgives, leads, and saves because he is God and does so as man, one person who unites in himself divinity and humanity. Appreciating the twofold and sometimes threefold rule with which Peter assumes is crucial if we are to understand how offices like "Leader and Savior" express Christ's person.

The Two Graces

There are two graces that Peter's speeches highlight, the forgiveness of sin and the gift of the Holy Spirit. As I hope I have made clear, these graces have a foundation, which is the mystery of Christ's person. Grace is of Christ, and Jesus Christ is of the Father. The grace that brings about new goodness has a trinitarian structure. We see this in the Father's actions with respect to the Son as the Father raises him. We are subject to the Son, in all his healing and saving, and this too is grace, made possible by the Father's sending. The forgiveness of sins is achieved by Christ's sacrifice, the gift of the Spirit of God being poured out by Jesus Christ, one person in whom divinity and humanity are personally united.

Peter's speech to Simon in Acts 8:20–24 is instructive. Simon's actions in trying to buy from the apostles the ability to "bestow" the Spirit's power on others is grist for the mill for considering grace in relation to Christ's person. Though the Spirit is a gift to us, the Spirit is proper to Christ's person. The grace that is the gift of the Spirit comes through Christ, but Christ himself, unlike us, does not have to obtain the gift of the Spirit, for he always sees the Father. Jesus does not serve the Father so as to obtain the Spirit. Jesus Christ does not have a part or share in the Spirit—as does the baptized believer—because Jesus is always one with the Spirit together with the Father. Even more, "because Christ's soul was united to his divinity," Jesus is more intimate to the Father and the Spirit than any other.[59] Jesus Christ is by nature God. That said, Jesus "did need to have grace in his human nature."[60] Jesus was a pilgrim. However, unlike Simon (or anyone else for that matter), Jesus did not need grace because of his heart being wicked; Jesus did not need grace because his heart was corrupt. Jesus likewise needs neither forgiveness nor leading, but Jesus does need grace in a certain respect. This raises the question: How can one who needs grace (in his humanity) give grace and be the fullness thereof? Thomas supplies an elegant answer, one that helps us receive Peter's speech to Simon. Christ has the fullness of grace because his soul "is joined more closely to God than other spiritual creatures." Christ is the complete opposite of Simon, who is "in the gall of bitterness and the chains of wickedness" (8:23). Jesus has "grace in full" because there is no other to whom the Holy Spirit bears witness as the Spirit does Christ.[61] As we have seen in previous sections, the ultimate reason as to why Christ has "the fullness of grace" is because "he is the only begotten of the Father."[62] Because he is eternally born of the Father, Jesus Christ blesses and baptizes with the Spirit, the gift of God. As one eternally born of the Father, Jesus shares with the Father the Holy Spirit. As one born of the virgin in "the fullness of time," he gives to us a share in the heavenly gifts he receives from the Father "such as vision, comprehension and enjoyment."[63] But he does not give these gifts if we are in bitterness and wickedness. Simon functions as a useful contrast to Christ, then. Jesus does not need grace because his heart is wicked; rather, Jesus needs grace because he is human, and to be human, as is Jesus, is to be perfected by grace, even if one is God's Son (cf. Luke 2:52). This is, I think, the only way to guarantee the full integrity of Jesus' humanity.

Let us press this inquiry further. Jesus is said to be anointed, as indicated in Peter's great speech in Acts 10:34–43 in the House of Cornelius, "with the Holy Spirit and with power." It is the anointed Christ who, in his great power, answers Peter's prayer for Simon, and it is Jesus Christ who enjoys, to the greatest degree, God being with him—"for God was with him" (10:38). God is with Jesus, enabling him to heal "all who were oppressed by the devil," and this because of the "grace of union" (10:38). The hypostatic union is a graced union. With this phraseology, we reach the heart of our account of the grace of Christ. Indeed, this little phrase—"the grace of union"—illuminates the metaphysics of the person—Jesus Christ—whom Peter preaches to Cornelius' household. When we contemplate what it is that Jesus is said to have done in Peter's extraordinary speech in 10:34–43, we see the extent to which those acts illustrate the "grace of union." Jesus does good, heals, and, as one ordained by God, judges the living and the dead. Jesus is "a kind of universal principle of grace," says

Thomas.[64] He is that because of his person, for the one person of Christ unites in himself divinity and humanity, and he unites them in such a way that our reception of him (in the least of these) becomes the means for our transformation.

Jesus Christ is such a "principle" because he is the eternal recipient of the Father's boundless generosity. Recall that the Son is, as the Father's eternally begotten, given the ultimate gift, "the divine nature which is an infinite gift."[65] Jesus gives to us just as generously as the Father gives to him; that is the basis for his generosity among us, expressed by those two great gifts, the forgiveness of sins and the gift of the Spirit. Jesus does not grasp the divine nature he receives but does good with it, healing those oppressed by the devil, and to those who believe, granting forgiveness of sins.

Grace's Purpose

What then is grace's purpose? If Christ in his grace forgives and gives the gift of the Spirit, what is then the *telos* of such giving? Grace achieves something extraordinary, the unity of "a thinking creature to God." Whether it be aspects of Peter's speech that highlight God's action in relation to Jesus—"but God raised him on the third day"—or action undertaken by Jesus himself, one truth stands out, namely that this person (Jesus Christ) enjoys "a union of person" with God (the Father) (Acts 10:40).[66] Jesus acts as he does because he is personally united with "the only begotten Son of the Father."[67] Israel's Messiah is the only begotten of God. This we can say of no other. Accordingly, Jesus is not occasionally united to God but "personally united to the Son of God."[68] Jesus is not a composite creature, a hybrid as it were. He is God's Son. Creatures, as creatures, require grace if they are to share in what is utterly above them. Grace unites what is human to what is divine.[69] In this sense, the man Jesus, as we have seen, receives grace. And what he receives—grace—he bestows, uniting us to God in such a way that "everyone who believes in him receives forgiveness of sins through his name" (10:43).

What is extraordinary about the narrative is that the grace that unites thinking creatures to God is for both Jews and Gentiles: "God shows no partiality" (Acts 10:34). Christ's rule, as Calvin reminds us, is being "extended to the Gentiles."[70] Even—or perhaps especially—there are those among the Gentiles who fear God and do right, Cornelius being exemplary. This is due to Christ's power, power that would, as Calvin reminds us, "draw the world, by the pleasant taste of goodness and kindness, to love Him and long for Him."[71] Amazingly, Peter thinks that the Gentile audience is capable of fearing God and doing what is right. Grace is present to all, even prior to Peter's preaching, effecting goodness everywhere, in the hearts of all those who fear God and do what is right. Grace, in terms of its direction to what is above us, does not diminish our nature but, instead, completes and perfects it.

Before we transition to thinking about grace in relationship to Christ as judge, let us think for a brief moment about the kind of agency Christ currently exercises. Though we have seen how God is very much the main agent in Peter's speeches, Jesus exercises a distinct form of agency by commanding. As with the speech to those in Jerusalem regarding the apostolic endeavors in Judea in Acts 10:34–43, we see Jesus at work. The first work Jesus does is command, and what he commands is preaching and testimony regarding God's having ordained him as "judge" (10:42). What are we to make of this, especially in relation to the grace of Christ just described? We must say that Jesus Christ encounters us as one who commands. There is not any command-free Christ, grace that is not clothed in command. The grace of Christ, if we are to honor its apostolic form, comes, in part, in the form of a command. All those who believe in him and receive the gift of the Spirit, whether they be Jews or Gentiles, receive the command to bear witness. While we are not all called to be preachers, we are all commanded to bear testimony to Jesus. The grace of Christ includes the command to testify to him as "judge of the living and the dead" (10:42). He indeed commands us to testify to him as judge.

Jesus is, however, ordained not by himself but by God, and his ordination by God is for a work, namely judgment. We have already heard about his leading and saving, but now we hear about his work as judge in Acts 10:42. He is present as the one who commands us to attest him as end-time judge. Whether one is a Jew, a Samaritan like Simon, or a Gentile, they will be judged by Jesus. Judgment is Jesus' work. Though future, he is present now commanding us to bear witness to this news. And what does he judge? Jesus judges whether we are worthy of the gospel, indeed, whether we believe. When we believe the apostolic message regarding his end-time judgment, however, we receive the grace of forgiveness through his name.

Grace, especially in terms of its being a work of God's mercy that expels defects, has a wide range. Peter's sermon attributes a specific work to Jesus—that is, judgment—and this work is relevant to all, Jews and Gentiles. Jesus will encounter us all as judge. The grace of Jesus Christ is in part the announcement of his judgment. Jesus does not encounter us as a mere man; instead, he will meet us as the judge of all humankind. That said, we whom he encounters at the end are not destitute of his grace—for, as grace, "he is Lord of all" (Acts 10:36). Jesus Christ, instead, recognizes every single person whether they be Jews, Samaritans, or Gentiles (like Cornelius), as one whom he will judge with respect to the message concerning himself. Jesus loves us as those whom he judges, addresses, and calls to belief. It is grace that we are judged by one who is the Lord and whose judgment originates not with ourselves but with God. God ordains as God does because God is good, showing no partiality. Christ is a judge who is good, healing "all who were oppressed by the devil" (10:38).

Accordingly, when we consider Christ's grace, we must also consider it in terms of not only the personal union but this twofold work of his, commanding and judging. We conclude this chapter by meditating upon how grace—the grace of union—is further illuminated in Peter's last speech (cf. Acts 15:7–11). Herein we discover afresh what Calvin calls the "whole substance of the

Gospel."[72] In Peter's last speech, we hear the word grace, "the grace of the Lord Jesus" (15:11). The use of the term, grace, makes especially good sense against the backdrop of the law, what Calvin calls the ceremonies. The law, specifically circumcision "according to the custom of Moses," is described in Peter's speech as a "yoke" (15:10). Not just circumcision, however, but "the law of Moses" is the issue. The problem with the law is that it is unbearable.

What renders the law of Moses, and more specifically its ceremonies, unbearable? The law of Moses is unbearable when received apart from Christ. The law is given to Moses by God. It is not deficient in terms of its original purpose, namely that of directing all facets of Israel's life in holiness to God. The problem, however, is that the law neither comes with nor supplies grace. We may not say "the grace of the law of Moses" whereas Peter says just that of Jesus—"the grace of Christ." The question arises, then, as to whether Jesus' grace lacks the law of Moses, especially the command to circumcise. It does not. Jesus' grace does not render the law null and void. Instead, as Calvin comments, the law has "perpetuity," meaning "the shadows of the Law" have been put to an end, "seeing that the perpetuity of the Law is founded on Christ."[73] Because of this, hearts cleansed by faith through the powerful working of the Spirit, whether they be Jew or Gentile, are saved *not* by adherence to the law. Faith fulfills the original aim of the law, purifying our hands. The law's original aim, then, is redeemed in Christ. The law orders the people of God to God, in holiness and righteousness, and this Jesus does as well. And yet, because grace is said of Christ, Christ orders us to God in an entirely supernatural way. His grace elevates us in such a way that we (whether Jew or Gentile) fulfill the spirit of the law; through the cleansing work of the Spirit, we believe and are saved, becoming God's people. The law's perpetuity is founded on Christ, insofar as the law teaches us to order our lives to God in holiness. This, Jesus does, but he also gives us what the law cannot give, which is to give us all that belongs to him including faith. Faith is a gift. The law encourages faith but does not give it. Jesus, however, gives us what is his, including his Spirit—the greatest gift—and faith. There is more, however: the Spirit who cleanses hearts by faith imparts through that faith what belongs to Christ. This too is grace; we receive what is his, including the grace of Sonship. We are in Christ adopted sons and daughters, not by nature but by grace, receiving Christ's benefits and a share in the life common to him, the Father and the Spirit.

Jesus, as grace, the good news itself, does far more than the law could ever do. He not only commends and teaches obedience, as does the law, but, unlike the law, he makes us faithful and obedient. Jesus elevates us, making us believers, whether we be Jews or Gentiles, and the means by which he does so is, in part, his command. This is where we understand the humbling function of law established upon Christ. While Calvin argues that the purpose of the law "is to humble men with the condemnation of eternal death," I think it is better to say that the law of Moses, whether in its original form or as founded on Christ, humbles not because of the threat of condemnation but because of God's grandeur.[74] The law points us to its Giver, who is God, a sense of whose majesty the law excites. God's grandeur not only points out our having fallen dramatically short of God, but God's grandeur is itself immensely desirable and good. What humbles persons and excites them to seek God is God's great and terrifying grandeur.

Conclusion

It is important in conclusion to step back for a moment and consider the theological gravity of what Peter is saying. Peter's concern is to set the stage straight as it were. As we reflect on the emergent Christology in Peter's sermons, three key questions are answered. The questions have to do with "whether He [Jesus] does exist, who He is, and what is His nature."[75] Jesus does exist. And we cannot understand his existence and reign without the Father. He exists and lives because "God raised him on the third day" (Acts 10:40). He exists eternally as the Father's only begotten Son, and he exists and ministers among us as the one whom the Father raises, commanding us to testify to his eschatological judgment. The question of his identity is, I think, quite straightforward. He is "the Lord" (11:16). That is his name, a name he shares with the Father and Spirit. This man is the Lord. When it comes to his nature, the designation we are given is grace. One name, above all else, is said *of* the Lord Jesus, and that is grace. This is true of the Son of Mary, "the mediator, whom God promised from the beginning."[76] Yes, this one is promised but, I would add, promised in the mode of the law of Moses, for, as Jesus says to the Jews in John's Gospel, "If you believed Moses, you would believe me, for he wrote about me" (5:46). The law promises one who will write the law on our hearts. Third and last, regarding his nature, we must say that he is gracious, for grace is of him. What grace makes possible is a work, the work of salvation. Christ's nature underwrites the work he, as man, undertakes, and his nature is from above, enjoying a creaturely participation in divinity in his one person. We participate through Jesus Christ in the goodness of the blessed Trinity. However, that grace and the salvation it accomplished is something we must seek. Calvin recognizes not only that the grace of the Lord Jesus saves (and will save) but also that it must be sought. Indeed, if we do not keep seeking it, we will inevitably domesticate it, so seek it we must, "the grace of the Lord" (15:40).

What we see, in part, as we contemplate the grace of the Lord Jesus is how it is both continuous with and discontinuous from the old covenant as represented by Moses' law. The point about continuity has much to do with gifts. The first gift of grace is the law. Without the law, we would not know what is clean and unclean; indeed we would not know God as the one who is above all gods. Such knowledge is above us. God tells his people so. The grace of the Lord Jesus does not disown the Jews and the law of Moses. Instead, it represents the fulfillment of God's determination to establish a people commensurate with the promise made to the Fathers.[77] God fulfills that promise and, in so doing, brings about the salvation of the Gentiles. God's secret purpose is present in the yoke given to the ancestors, for that yoke contains the hint of a call relating to the inclusion of the Gentiles into God's family. Acceptance of that call assumes, moreover, daily cleansing: Christ, as Calvin says, works "daily destroying our sins, for which He once made atonement by His blood."[78] As with the ceremonies, cleansing is the aim. But instead of being cleansed by Moses-inspired acts of obedience, we are cleansed from the inside out by faith. Faith in God's gift through the Holy Spirit, enabling us to fulfill the only law there is, "the Law of Christ" (Gal 6:2), the very *telos* of Moses' law.

In sum, the grace of the ascended Lord Jesus Christ is present. Jesus Christ enjoys a personal union with divinity and is present to us, humanly speaking. In his one person, the person of God's beloved Son, divinity and humanity are united. Peter's speeches encourage us to receive Christ as one who communicates himself to us freely in faith, blessing us with the grace of union, cleansing us and daily renewing us in his Spirit. Grace's form is Christ, and its pattern is the law, though unlike the law, Jesus would have us rely on himself as the one in whom the law is founded and completed, not only for Jews but for Gentiles as well. Looking ahead, we see that the grace of Christ is never without the powerful and secret working of his Spirit, the Spirit whom Calvin calls "the Governor and Director of the faithful."[79] This has been assumed but not developed. As we journey in a more explicitly pneumatological direction, however, we will not leave Christ behind, to say nothing of God's mercy, for we learn, as one contemplates the pneumatological dimensions of Peter's speeches, the extent to which the Spirit communicates to the faithful what "applies to His [Christ's] own person."[80]

3

The Hope of the Spirit

n this chapter, I explore hope in connection with the Holy Spirit. I shed some light on hope, specifically, "the hope of blessed immortality."[1] I do so in a way that also seeks to do justice to hope in the present and indeed to hope's comprehensiveness as a theological theme. I think about immortality as the *telos* of the Spirit's work of regeneration, and I consider heaven as the direction of the Spirit's rule and, of course, miracles and the light they shed on the hope of blessed immortality. While our reflection, then, in this chapter is directed primarily to the future, what John Webster calls the "backward reference" always remains in view, for we connect the Spirit in mission among us and the work the Spirit accomplishes therein with the Spirit's procession from the Father as "Love" and "Gift."[2]

The Acts of the Apostles, as I have been arguing, is a most theocentric book. The principal agent, actor, and person in the narrative is God (the Father). This is not to detract, for a moment, from Calvin's insight that the book "originated from the Spirit Himself."[3] The Spirit is an important divine agent in the narrative and in the narrative's inspired production in the hands of Luke.[4] Though the emphasis in the book is primarily on God, a rich theocentric account of the Spirit is present. Peter's speeches instruct us regarding the Spirit's ministry of renewing the people of God, the culmination of that renewal being heavenly bliss, blessed immortality in which both Jews and, astonishingly, Gentiles may participate. Let us begin, then, by giving attention to the grace of the Spirit.

The Metaphysics of the Spirit

Calvin refers to the "grace of the Spirit" as the most excellent gift, indeed that "all else is worth nothing without this." What makes the gift—the Spirit's grace—so excellent, especially in light of the fact that we have just finished a chapter on Christ's grace? Because the Spirit "opens to us the door for us to enter all the treasures of spiritual blessings."[5] The door the Spirit makes known is Christ.[6] Christ is raised up by God, and the outcome of that is the gift of the Spirit poured out—"this that you both see and hear" (Acts 2:33). Even here, metaphysics is not very far away, and so we ought to discuss the Spirit in relation to Father and Son. The Spirit is *from* the Father, but from the Father who eternally bears a Son who too receives (eternally) the Spirit from the Father. What happens here in time—the Spirit poured out—is a repetition in time of the eternal mystery of the triune life. The Son receives (always) the Spirit from the Father, and what he receives in his resurrection afresh—the Spirit who raises him—he communicates to us. The greatest gift of the resurrected and ascended Christ is what the Father pours out through him, the Holy Spirit. Though the Spirit is ordered to the Father, the Spirit, as with the Son, is equal to him. Order, accordingly, does not imply inequality. The Spirit is divine as one who proceeds from the Father.

If such is the case, then, the Father is from no one. The Father is from himself and the Spirit from the Father as is the case with the Son, the Father's only begotten. This is the teaching of Acts. Although we do not say that the Son proceeds as does the Spirit, for the Son is begotten of the Father, we do affirm that the Spirit is sent by the Son or through the Son, the Son whom the Spirit declares. That said, there is, as Mascall notes, "no fourth Person in the Godhead to reveal or interpret the Spirit."[7] The Spirit interprets the Son and in him the Father. The Father, furthermore, enjoys an immediate originating relation with the Spirit, and the Son (the Lord Jesus) a mediate relationship in that the Son has the Spirit from the Father. This helps us to make sense of Peter's direction to the "brothers" in his Pentecost speech in Acts 2:38–39. God the Father moves in repentant hearts subject to baptism by "the gift of the Holy Spirit" so that the name of Jesus Christ may take root within us (2:38). The promise—the gift of the Spirit—is for those whose ancestors' apostasy the Spirit foretold through David. The promise is indeed too much for those who are near and so is directed to "all those who are far away" (2:39). And the promise of the Father, the Holy Spirit, is, as with grace itself, above us, not representative of any kind of potential within us. As Mascall writes, "the doctrine of the Holy Spirit (in contrast to the dazzling manifestation of the Son) . . . has the character of a secret, a partially revealed tradition." Mascall continues, the Spirit "nevertheless remains himself undisclosed and hidden, concealed by the deity which he reveals to us, by the gift which he imparts."[8]

How can this be? It can only be because of God. God fills not only the preached message with his Spirit—his great gift—but also those who preach that message; Peter and his message are Spirit filled. As Willie Jennings notes of Peter's Pentecost sermon, "Peter's sermon exists only within the Holy Spirit."[9] In words as arresting as they are clear, Calvin writes of Peter and John (and of believers as a whole, but especially of Peter and John) that they are "men in whom the Spirit of God was manifest with a singular efficacy and power."[10] The message advances as it does not on the apostles' own steam but rather via the power of the Spirit, the Spirit who does not dispense with them—for that is not how God works. Instead, the Spirit "rules in the Church through the apostles."[11] The Spirit succeeds among us not by displacing but by ruling via our witness. The success of the apostles and the flourishing of their message is because "the Spirit of the living God breathed on their witness."[12] The Spirit's rule, of course, does not eclipse the form of Christ: the Spirit's rule has cruciform shape. The Spirit leads us to Christ, yes, but to the Christ who died and was raised. And so the prayers for boldness on the part of Peter and the Spirit's filling lead to the cross, indeed, for courage to "carry it when it is laid upon us."[13]

The Law and the Spirit

Having launched our treatment of the Spirit by briefly considering the Spirit in relation to the Father and Son, we need to think about how the greatest gift of the new covenant relates to the old covenant, specifically the law. One of the blessings of the cross of Christ—and of grace more broadly—is that it restores us to a right relationship with the law of Moses as encapsulated by the Ten Commandments. Jesus puts to death unspiritual uses of the law. An ungodly, indeed an unspiritual, reception of the law is one in which the law's "reality" and "substance" are ignored.[14] The law's principle is the Spirit. Calvin reminds us that the "power and effect [of the ceremonies] depend solely on the Spirit of God."[15] Why is that? Because without the interior ministry of the Spirit, we cannot understand the origins of Moses' law and the law's function as that which prepares us to receive Christ. However, the law, when obeyed in the Spirit, leads us Godward. The law cannot fulfill its purpose, then, without the Spirit, and anything to do with the Spirit leads us closer to and not further away from God. The Spirit confirms the source of the law is that of God himself. And yet in confirming the law as from God, the Spirit transfigures the law, disclosing its heart—God—in a way that moves us to Christ, whose law is the only law there is.[16] The law does not detract from Christ but points, in the Spirit, toward him, who is its fulfillment.

The inability of Israel's leadership to see the law's substance is part and parcel with the rejection of its own Messiah. Acceptance of Jesus Christ as Israel's Messiah opens Israel afresh to its own law, its spiritual origins. Rather than simply being an instrument by which Israel's exterior life is organized, the law, when received spiritually, engraves the divine presence on our hearts in such a way that we fear sinning against God and love him less than we ought. The Spirit lifts up our eyes, granting us faith in order that we might see whose law this is, and how it, as with the created order itself, bears the presence and imprint of its Creator. The law—as with all gifts—is expanded by the Spirit such that the law bears Christ's voice.[17] It is as if the law now declares to us in the Spirit that its *telos* is Christ. The Spirit is gift, and as a result of the gifts of the Spirit, we are able to receive all that comes from God as gift, including the law.

This is not to say, however, that there are not greater and lesser gifts in God's economy. Yes, the Spirit is the law's "substance," but the law does not gift us with the Spirit as does the gospel. We are not the Spirit's governor and director, thankfully, though when we open ourselves to Christ the Spirit becomes our governor and director. The Spirit's ministry and the hope the Spirit gives never stand on their own. This is seen most powerfully, I think, in Peter's address to Cornelius' house in Acts 10:34–43 and to the Hebrews in 15:7–11. Peter celebrates the faith of the Gentiles, which is of course Spirit inspired. The Gentiles' embrace of the gospel, accompanied as it is by the Spirit's descent, shows us what Calvin calls "the harmony of the eternal word and secret power of the Spirit." As Luke writes, "the Holy Spirit fell upon all who heard the word" (10:44). "Faith comes from what is heard," and what is heard is the good news, the good news that includes the regenerative power of the Spirit, the Gentile confession of which shows us the "harmony" between the preached word and the Spirit's power (Rom 10:17).[18]

The Spirit leads to God but only through the word. Though the law was not intended for Gentiles, the gospel that blesses us with the Spirit is intended for them, to say nothing of the Jew, following Romans 1:16. Messianic Israel includes Gentiles upon whom the Spirit has been poured out. The relationship between Jews and Gentiles has, once and for all, been remade; "the dividing wall, that is, the hostility between us," has been cast down (Eph 2:14), though not in such a way that Gentiles, as per Acts 15:29, ought not restrain themselves in relationship to four things, for example, food "sacrificed to idols." Such food may be stumbling blocks for their Jewish brothers and sisters. Even such modest restrictions, however, do not detract from the great grace of the Spirit that has fallen on the Gentiles thereby expanding "the space of Israel."[19] The law of Moses, whose origins are spiritual, leads to Jesus, who reconciles Jews and Gentiles to the Father, pouring out the Spirit upon the same.

Hope and Apostasy

We are created by God and for God, even more, "to become," as Basil notes, "like God, as far as this is possible for human nature."[20] Our desire as human beings is, or, if not, ought to be, for God, though we so often corrupt the natural desire for God by worshiping created things in place of the Creator. As we read Peter's and especially Stephen's synopses of Israel's history, it is immediately apparent that human nature, the nature of those—but not just those—with whom God covenants, is averse to God, to desiring and becoming like him, let alone "becoming God."[21] In the face of the outright hostility that Stephen describes in his sprawling speech in Acts 7:1–53 or that Paul in his first speech in 13:16–41 notes, especially verses 27–29, is there any salience to what Basil argues? I think there is, and the reason there is has to do with God. The speeches help us to see this. "God was kind and generous to them [the Jews]," Calvin comments, "one might say despite themselves, when they were fighting against Him."[22] God never ceases to be near a "stiff-necked people"; God never ceases to touch us, despite ourselves (7:51). God is near them but in a way hidden from them. Take, for example, the law as a mode of God's commanding and directing presence. To be sure, God turns "away from them and hands them over to worship the host of heaven" (7:42), as Stephen recounts insofar as they forsake God's law, yet even in turning away, God is present albeit hidden in the form of prophetic speech in the voice of, for example, Israel. And here we must consider the Spirit, for the violence of Israel's history—their pushing God "aside"—is directed, says Stephen, toward "the Holy Spirit" (7:39, 51). Indeed, Israel's antipathy to the law is ultimately directed to the Spirit, the law's reality.

The Holy Spirit, as with Father and Son, is boundless, but in a way unique to the hypostatic subsistence of the Spirit. The Spirit—"the wind blows where it chooses" (Acts 3:8)—is not "contained in any spatial limits."[23] This is not true of the Son, though it is true of the Father. That is important for understanding Stephen's judgment about Israel's opposition being opposition to the Spirit. The Spirit is God, and so to oppose the Spirit is to oppose God. The Spirit is one with the essence of God; the person of the Spirit has the character of substance; the three are consubstantial.[24] God's essence is not in any sense prior to the subsisting relationship that is the person of the Spirit. And so, when Israel opposes the Spirit, it opposes the "I am" who appeared to Moses; it also closes its ears to prophetic speech and ignores the law's substance.

In an extraordinary move, Stephen casts (in Acts 7:51) the whole of Israel's sordid history as opposition to the Spirit and those who God sends, for example, Moses and the prophets. Why does Stephen say the Spirit and neither the Father nor the Son? That has, I think, to do with the sense that in the Old Testament Israel's opposition is directed, primarily, to the mouthpieces of the Spirit, Moses and the prophets, for it is through them that the Spirit speaks. Recall the Creedal language: "We believe in the Holy Spirit, the Lord, the giver of life, who proceeds from the Father and the Son, who in unity with the Father [and the Son], is worshiped and glorified, and has spoken through the prophets." Recall, too, Peter's words in 1:16 regarding the Spirit's foretelling through David of Judas' apostasy. David is also one through whom the Spirit speaks, a prophet as it were. Spatial limits are not appropriate to the Spirit because of the Spirit's essence or divinity, concealed as the Spirit is "by the deity which he reveals to us."[25] God is not circumscribed, and this is especially true of God in the person of God's Spirit. The metaphysical basis of the Spirit as being the person of God to whom Israel's resistance is directed is the Spirit's essence, an essence common to three, an essence infinite and boundless. Here, as elsewhere, careful reference to the unity of the divine essence and the Trinity of persons is necessary.

In greater detail, the Spirit will never become incarnate; that is not, of course, the form of the Spirit's mission among us; the Son is incarnate. The Pauline motif of "in the fullness of time" does not apply to the Spirit, for the Spirit is there present in the beginning of Israel's history in a way that is unique to the Spirit himself (Gal 4:4).[26] Overcoming of spatial and temporal distance is, in part, the Spirit's speciality, which is why, for example, the elevating work of the Spirit is so crucial to the faithful's partaking of the ascended Christ in bread and wine at that great heavenly banquet, the Eucharist. Accordingly, whether it be the prophet Habakkuk, Jeremiah, or Moses, it is the Spirit that is being opposed in Israel's opposition to them. The Spirit does not replace the prophets upon whom the Spirit alights; likewise, the Spirit does not compete with them, but the Spirit does receive the vitriol directed to them. If such is the case, then, even Israel's opposition is recognized as opposition only in relation to God. The Spirit's lack of any spatial limits—a comment on the Spirit's person, the Spirit's distinct mode of being God—is the basis for the Spirit receiving opposition via the prophets who bear the Spirit's voice. The boundless Spirit, though not contained, is nonetheless profoundly intimate to the prophets, speaking through them and receiving (albeit impassibly) the fury directed toward them. This does not render the Spirit a composite creature: the Spirit is not merged with them. The Spirit remains transcendent of them and yet immediately present to them.

The Spirit's foretelling ministry and the Spirit's receiving of prophetic opposition point to an elementary truth about the Spirit. The Spirit is other-directed, that is, to the Father and thus the Son. The Spirit does not foretell the Spirit's self but "the Righteous One" (Acts 7:52). So Mascall again: "The Spirit's economy within the Church is to be the interpreter of the Son."[27] Similarly, the Spirit does not lift up our eyes so as to see the Spirit's self. The harmony of the Father, Son, and Spirit relationship is seen in the

Spirit's raising our vision heavenward to "the glory of God and Jesus at the right hand of God" (7:35). The Spirit excels in disturbing spatial limits, for in being filled with the Spirit, Stephen, while on earth, sees heaven opened and Jesus exalted at God's right hand. The Spirit, in showing Stephen heaven, shows us the pattern of "Christian prayer," "living," and worship—"*To* the Father, *through* the Son, *in* the Spirit."[28] We look to the Father in the Spirit through the Son. The metaphysical basis of the vision is apparent: Stephen's gaze is toward the Father and Son, for the Spirit is from them, and so the Spirit lifts our vision to them by relativizing limits that we think of as simply self-evident: a strict bifurcation of heaven and earth, things invisible and visible.

Thinking about this some more, the Son is located in a place that the Spirit is not because he (the Son) is at the Father's side. This is not to say that the Father's side is a circumscribed place. He descends from there and ascends to there. But the Spirit's 'possession' of Godhead is different, not in any essential sense, but simply by virtue of the Spirit's being "love proceeding," in God and among us, following the logic of John 17:26.[29] It is love for his people that causes God to oppose them as God does, indeed for the sake of the promise made to Abraham. It is not as if God has failed because his church lies "oppressed under tyranny" of its own making, but it is to say that God is powerfully present in the midst of tyranny through Spirit-empowered prophetic opposition.[30] Just as when tyranny reaches its climax in the closed ears and shouts of those rushing Stephen, the Spirit is present, doing what the Spirit has always done, that is, showing us the Messiah either standing—or sitting—at God's right hand. The inner harmony of the three persons is most wonderfully beheld in the apostasy culminating in Stephen's martyrdom. Even the order of the persons one to another is, as it were, beheld, for Stephen sees, first, God's glory, which is only befitting because the Spirit proceeds from the Father; but Stephen also sees the Son of Man standing there, for the Spirit comes and is sent through him. And to whom does the Spirit in Stephen return? The Spirit, whom Stephen gives up, just as Jesus did in Luke 23:46, is returned to Jesus, not surprisingly, for the Spirit brings us back to the Father through the Lord Jesus.

Summing up this section, when we think about apostasy, we must think about the Spirit, for it is the Spirit to whom Israel's opposition is directed.[31] Apostasy is intelligible in relation to the Spirit, who shows us how resistance to him—as resistance to Moses and the prophets—is also resistance to the God and Father of our Lord Jesus Christ. The gift of the Spirit to the Gentiles, a gift that shows us God's love for all people, even more a people who are not his elect—that is, the Gentiles—is the basis for our thinking about the hope of the Spirit and its culmination in blessed immortality. Just so, without a strong sense of the metaphysics of the Spirit and how the Spirit is the substance of Israel's law and the object of Israel's resistance, we are unable adequately to apprehend the precious hope the Spirit inspires. The hope of the Spirit anticipates "blessed immortality."[32]

Hope

What must we say about hope? Peter's last speech to the council in Acts 15:7–11 instructs us. Hope relates to what God has done by gifting the Gentiles with the Spirit. Hope has reference to, as Jennings puts it, God's "tastes [being] much wider than Peter had imagined until this moment."[33] The ultimate end-time gift is given to the Gentiles, meaning that God's people have been radically expanded and reconstituted anew by that same gift. What right-thinking Jew would have ever thought that God's people would have been so renewed as to include non-Jews while never obviating the priority of the Jew in God's covenantal purposes and plans? Jewish believers ought to include Gentile Christians in their fellowship, indeed as brothers and sisters, and that this is so is cause for wonder, then, at God's taking pleasure in doing such a new thing. And the hope given here is, not surprisingly, God-centered. The hope of the Spirit is hope in God, God who urges his believing people "to explore unknown paths," to see that at the heart of their life is "a paradigm shift."[34] The path along which the Spirit would take us is God, the God "who knows the human heart" (15:8). But the path or way to God is through Jesus, crucified, raised, and ascended. And Jesus, whose grace saves, compels the brothers to make "no distinction between them and us" (15:9). Here lie the contours of hope: the Spirit takes us into Israel's history, allowing us to see the law for what it is, "a yoke" (15:10). It is a positive yoke, however, for it comes from God, has its reality in God's Spirit, and directs toward God. It is a yoke that never stands on its own, for it is God's law, and there is nothing that God creates and sustains in being—including the law of Moses—that is not subject to God's perfecting work in the Spirit. Even disasters—and Israel's history is an "uninterrupted spiritual disaster"—can, and so often are, remade by him.[35]

More specifically, the hope of the Spirit is, in part, that the gulf between Jew and Gentiles has been bridged by God. Acts tells us that Gentiles are turning to God; God's restoration of his people involves their inclusion.[36] The word of the Lord, either proclaimed in the synagogues and congregations of first-century Asia Minor or by others in the twenty-first century, is a word that relativizes hard-and-fast distinctions of space and time. God sets apart today men and women through whom the word is proclaimed and heard, the word through which the Spirit is given. The Holy Spirit is continually poured out, the hope being that the Christian church and tradition will in light of that continually live and grow, till Christ comes again, to the glory of the Father. The hope of the Spirit is that the Christ who spoke to Saul on the Damascus road will speak, as he promises, in his assembly today, enabling his body to preserve unity with the message spoken by Peter to "the apostles and elders" regarding God's relationship to Gentile flesh (Acts 15:6).

God's call to forsake yokes—which is really anything received apart from the Spirit—is a call that is effective. This too is grounds for hope. Calvin indeed draws attention to the Word's efficacy when describing the call or illumination of the Spirit. While I do not think the effectual character of the call should be limited to "only those he has determined to save," as Calvin does, I do think the Spirit's call to faith always bears fruit.[37] The language of the Spirit's falling in Acts 10:4 does not allow the believing community to be complacent with respect to well-trodden paths, for God and his purposes are not ours to capture. God does nonetheless have those who are his, whose identity as such is known to God alone. Therefore we have reason to hope that a steadfast commitment to a "transcendent monotheism" fosters appreciation for God's "universal fatherhood." God delights in calling forth praise from those his people generally deem furthest away from God, people thought to be most unreachable and stubborn.[38]

A participatory approach, informed by the deep logic of Acts, validates such a monotheism. As Davison notes, "at the heart of creaturehood is the dynamic of *receiving* being, of having it by participation."[39] The yoke that Gentiles are to forsake is that of realizing themselves, of giving up what prevents them from being as "fully realised as what a thing can be."[40] The hope of the Spirit, for Gentiles and Jews, is that our "prayers" and "alms" (10:44) do not ascend to God on their own strength. God realizes them. God, knowing no potential, ability, or capacity to develop, answers prayers. It is not within the capacity of those praying to realize what they are praying for. And yet, the very act of praying evokes hope. Prayer in Acts 10 is a means by which those to be redeemed (Cornelius and his household) learn to see through creaturely things to their source. Cornelius' prayer and alms evoke a "forward orientation."[41] Hope has this character. God acts in response to Cornelius' prayers, summoning a certain Peter to appear. The journey Cornelius embarks upon is, ultimately, redemptive. It anticipates "the life of the world to come" wherein "the redeemed apprehend creaturely things in God, or through God."[42] Cornelius' form of life strengthens a participatory account of creatures' relationship to God. It makes sense of Cornelius' action—that he sees God as it were through his life and the life of the poor, receiving them in relation to God.[43]

Hope is enriched by a participatory understanding of the structure of creation. Created things are causes in such a way that traces of their cause remain in them, however grievous their sin.[44] A causal account of the God/world relation goes hand in hand with participation understood with reference to God's unicity. Traces in creatures—and here I also demure from Sonderegger—are reducible to the one divine essence common to the three persons.[45] The presence of vestiges, which Cornelius shows via his fear of and devotion toward God, turns us Godward. As Davison helpfully writes, "whatever of excellence is in a creature was in God first, and the name we give to the trace of that excellence in creatures can be used to imitate that excellence in God."[46] This makes sense of Cornelius' devotion and should inspire hope. God is a preservative cause. God preserves creatures in such a way that their excellences, however oblique, refer to him as their exemplary. Accordingly, hope is not to be thought of simply in eschatological terms. Hope relates also to God's causality. God causes creatures who are not bereft of vestiges. These vestiges demonstrate God's presence to what he causes, and that God causes creatures that exist in him and who are to be taken seriously as such. This gives hope.

A subtle but key point arises here. Davison, following Thomas' lead, makes clear how important it is to affirm that God is not in things "as part of their essence but as upholding them in being."[47] Hope relates to God perfecting in the life of the world to come what he now holds in being. Here too I find Sonderegger's insistence that the God/world relation is better characterized by "*indwelling*" rather strange.[48] Cornelius' pattern of life does not so much reflect God's indwelling—at least prior to the Spirit falling upon him—as opposed to God being in him and upholding him. I do not think we would say God indwells this devout man, but I do think we would say that God is in him, upholding him in being. Indwelling denotes a level of intimacy and intensity reserved for baptism in the Spirit and its corollary water baptism.

What is extraordinarily clear, moreover, as we consider the apostolic witness to God, and in particular God's Spirit, centered around Jerusalem as it is in the first half of the book of Acts, is the noncompetitive character of the Spirit's voice and work among us. The Spirit speaks through David, the whole of the prophets, and is happy to do so "secretly," to use a preferred idiom of Calvin's. Commenting on the witness of Scripture as a whole, Calvin writes that Scripture "unites the ministry of men with the secret inspiration of the Spirit."[49] The Spirit, in ministering through the likes of Peter, does not use Peter as a puppet of sorts. Though the Spirit speaks in a way that cannot be mistaken for gastronomic displeasure, the Spirit does not violate the creaturely integrity of the speeches. Men like Peter speak, and the Spirit unites their ministry to himself. Similarly, the Gentile Pentecost makes the Gentiles—Cornelius' household—into believers but does not, in so doing, obliterate their status as Gentiles even as it does involve the loss of their autonomy with respect to their Jewish brethren. They remain Gentiles, that is, non-Jews, though in spiritual and bodily communion with them in Jesus Christ. Accordingly, the Spirit is transcendent with respect to those whose ministry the Spirit unites to the Spirit's self. Think, for example, of the Spirit's directive to Philip: "Go over to this chariot and join it" (Acts 8:29). Philip hears the Spirit speak, while the eunuch does not. And yet, the Spirit does act in ways that are not necessarily quiet and secret: after all, the "Spirit of the Lord" snatches Philip away. But even then, Philip is snatched away in order that he might proclaim the good news elsewhere, to the towns in the region of Azotus. But again, Philip is propelled by God to preach elsewhere, and yet, of Philip's own accord, he "follows the lead of the Spirit," a leading that is due to God's Spirit in concert with Philip's own volition.[50] As Kathryn Tanner says so well, God's agency is "comprehensive of the whole [of the created order] and without essential relation to its effects by either simple identity or opposition."[51] So: the Spirit does not violate creaturely efforts to proclaim the good news but instead secretly unites them to himself, such that there might be harmony between the one ministering and the Spirit himself. Hope lies here. The transcendent Spirit promises involvement in our efforts. The Spirit does not add to our efforts; likewise the Spirit does not override them. However, the Spirit may—and herein lies the miraculous—bring about "created effects without sufficient created causes for them."[52] Again, the Spirit snatches Philip away.

The Holy Spirit is a scriptural Spirit. Accordingly, I think it is right to say that the "Spirit leads and directs believers' judgments from no other source than the Scriptures."[53] We know that the Spirit is at work if believers are drawn to patient listening to the Scriptures, if there is indeed a deep desire to proceed scripturally, to act in a way otherwise unintelligible apart from the Scriptures. The Spirit does not encourage a wooden devotion to the Scriptures, but, as Peter discovered at Cornelius' house, things previously thought scripturally unlawful—a Jew associating with a Gentile—are interpreted, by the gift of the Spirit poured out, lawful. What Peter discovered is that God is the Lord of all scriptural distinctions—"but God has shown me that I should not call anyone profane or unclean" (Acts 10:28). This does not devalue the Scriptures but is, instead, a simple reminder that we receive them in the Spirit. Herein lies our hope: God, in drawing us to himself, draws us to the Scriptures, that we might make judgments befitting God's purposes by the power of God's Spirit. And such judgments will always be judgments that "make us sharers in Christ's death and resurrection."[54] The Spirit leads and directs with respect to Scripture with a single purpose in view, namely, that of our inhabiting of Christ in his death and resurrection, our only hope. The Spirit moves us to the Scriptures, establishing us in a living relationship to them, one subject to God's purposes.

One last point before we think explicitly about the eschatological form of hope. One cannot but help think that Peter—the same Peter who declared to Jesus three times his love for him—had the ministry he had, at least in part, because Peter felt the presence of God's Spirit (cf. John 21:15–19).[55] Peter knows that sloth is the enemy as it were of feeling God's presence, and so the energy that characterizes Peter's ministry, and the boldness shown even when arrested as recorded in Acts 12:1–19, has at least some recourse to feeling. Peter, I suspect, feels and experiences God's direction, in part, because the Spirit has filled him in such a way that he is at peace with Jesus' words to him in John's Gospel: "But when you grow old, you will stretch out your hands, and someone else will fasten a belt around you and take you where you do not wish to go" (John 21:18). Peter knows this, recognizing that "the power of the Spirit is diffused throughout all parts of the world," giving him the confidence to be a criminal and martyr, for Peter cannot go where the Spirit is not.[56] The world, however damaged it may be, is not immune to the powerful presence and agency of the Spirit. The presence "in every nation" of those who fear God and do "what is right" is (again) evidence of this comprehensive agency (Acts 10:35). The Spirit is the preservative Spirit—"by the wonderful activity and instigation of his Spirit God preserves all that He has created out of nothing."[57] Creation includes preservation. Peter's apostolic calls include the promise of Christ's direction, even unto death. This insight indeed applies at the level of the upholding of all the apostles. God, who created them ex nihilo by raising Jesus, preserves them, too, and that by the Spirit.

It is through the Spirit that we make progress in what Calvin calls "the school of God."[58] That same Spirit, and his secret power, falls upon us in water baptism, enabling us to be the kind of person for whom the words spoken of Barnabas are spoken of us as well—"for he was a good man, full of the Holy Spirit and faith" (Acts 11:24). Such a person feels the Spirit, not in any romantic way, but simply because she sees Jesus. The filling of the Spirit is so comprehensive that we need not shy away from the language of feeling. The God we meet in the narrative would have us feel his love, feel his caress as it were on our flesh in baptism both in water and in the Spirit.[59] The hope presented to us in Acts in general and in Peter's speeches in particular, centered as they are around Jerusalem, is deeply disruptive. It is, however, a disruption for the sake of continuity: God is faithful to the promise, though in the most surprising of ways. The God of Israel shows himself to be one who expands Israel's space by the Spirit, granting life to a people hitherto deemed to be not his people in order that the promise be fulfilled. The same God also expands individuals like Peter, infusing them with feeling regarding the things of God, rendering them ever increasingly transparent to the God on whom they depend and whom they love.

Blessed Immortality

Here, not surprisingly, we gain a glimpse of why it is fitting to talk about blessed immortality in relationship to the Spirit. This now familiar chorus to us—"God raised up" (Acts 13:37)—is relevant to thinking with Peter about the Spirit. The Spirit raises our vision and gaze Godward, heavenward. One of the corollaries of the believer's being raised up heavenward is the anticipated experience of a total lack of corruption—Jesus is our exemplar here. Jesus, as Paul notes in his first speech, "experienced no corruption" (13:37). The hope of blessed immortality is just that: the hope of experiencing no corruption. Such an experience "exceeds altogether the created capabilities of human beings."[60] This is the hope and the eschatological blessing to which God calls us, the goal of God's work among us in the here and now. And its source and agent are the Spirit, who, as the Spirit did with Stephen, lifts the gaze heavenward to where Christ is, where there is no corruption. Blessed immortality is coextensive with the resurrected Christ, who, in the Spirit, shares what he has with us, uncorrupted life. It is that life that we live into here and now by the Spirit, also by God's mercy and Christ's grace. All told, this is "nothing else but the beginning of glory in us."[61]

Blessed immortality's center is Christ, but as with all things its foundation is God, for God raised Christ up, and in him God will one day raise us up too in such a way that we hope to see what Stephen saw.[62] Blessed immortality, the hope of experiencing no corruption, is, as with the promise made to the fathers, entirely God's doing. God—the source and root of all blessing—lifts our gaze through his Spirit in such a way that we might "see Jesus," the "pioneer and perfecter of our faith" (Heb 2:9, 12:2). May our vision be transparent to Jesus—that is our hope.

"Blessed immortality" is really the culmination of what Calvin calls the second part of the gospel, namely, "that they [believers] are fashioned again in newness of life by the Spirit of regeneration."[63] That life in which believers are fashioned is Christ, who is life itself. He is not a likeness of God but the image of God. The life the Spirit gives is the life of Christ, and his life is that of God himself. Blessed immortality is our receiving without end, in ever-increasing intensity, the life of Jesus Christ, a life common to him, the Father and their Spirit, such that God may be "all in all" (1 Cor 15:28)—"*To* the Father, *through* the Son, *in* the Spirit."[64]

Blessed immortality, it goes without saying, also "involves flesh."[65] It involves the presence of our flesh—flesh without corruption—before the Lord, in spatio-temporal presence to himself. This assumes "seeing what the LORD is."[66] In Paul Griffiths' astute words, blessed immortality, which is the defining characteristic of creaturely participation in heaven, is beatitude: "Heaven, the LORD as our timespace, is our beatitude, which is our glorious last thing, the *novissimum* for which we were made."[67] By "*novissimum*," Griffiths means that heaven as state and condition (of sorts) is never succeeded by something fresher, better, newer. It is a state, to once again use Griffiths' idiom, free of the "metronome," and a condition that is "immaculable, incapable of self-performed and self-inflicted sin."[68] Blessed immortality is heaven perfected and earth healed, heaven and earth reunited, the experience of no corruption, the Spirit indwelling us in ever-increasing intensity, that we might behold the lamb, to the glory of the Father. The Spirit enables this holding as the great gift, "the promise of the Father" poured out upon us in such a way that we (begin) to flee from sin and, however obliquely, anticipate our end when what the Lord is and has shall be "all in all" (1 Cor 15:27).[69]

This, too, I think lends itself to a participatory perspective. Immortality denotes the creatures real sharing, as a creature, in God.[70] Here, too, I question Sonderegger's championing of words like "Revolution" to describe God—"the Revolution who is God."[71] I appreciate what she is trying to honor—God's liveliness, God as "*cauterizing fire*," indeed "the utterly unpredictable and savage Holiness of the Lord God of Israel."[72] It is of course important to honor God as *Actus Purus*, as one who eternally reposes in the fiery act of being he eternally is. However, I am not convinced that Sonderegger's utilization of such terms as "Revolution" to indicate God's liveliness has adequate capacity to support a fulsome doctrine of creation.[73]

Sonderegger is at pains to communicate that God's nature is his relationship to the world, but we are left unsure as to why there is a world in the first place. Participation as a motif, when tied to a "substance-wise" register, goes a long way toward not only securing the basis for creation in God but also how creation's perfection—and therewith the creature's—"share the same underlying metaphysics."[74] There is a world because God wills that there be one, and because his will is one with and simple in him, it is a good world that God creates. What befits the goodness of God is a world that participates in and receives his goodness. The things God causes, God sustains. In a covenantal register, God creates Israel out of nothing via the promise, and God is faithful to the promise without remainder. Blessed immortality represents the culmination of the blessings intrinsic to the promise, the redemption of a people called to be God's ambassadors and intimates. Put differently, the God/world relationship requires a foundation, and that is divine goodness, and goodness that is communicable, shareable with creatures. What is said of God substance-wise is the metaphysical basis for creation's participatory character, for God's providence, redemption, and the eschatological perfection of the creature in the light of the world to come, blessed immortality. Talk of God as "Event," while not necessarily hostile to a more participatory account of the world and its foundation in God, makes articulation of the underlying metaphysical structure of creation much more difficult than it need be.[75]

The doctrine of revelation—our being shown something—is heavily present in Sonderegger. What I think Acts strongly intimates is an account of God and creation wherein we are not simply shown things. Rather, we, as Stephen exemplifies, learn to apprehend "all of reality, and all of our experience, in relationship to God" with the help of things God has made.[76] We, too, hope to one day see Jesus, even him standing as a reward for our receiving our lives in relationship to God, and receiving them as participations in God's eternal life.

Conclusion

To sum up this chapter, we considered the Spirit's metaphysics, indeed how they give us a purchase on Israel's law and render intelligible Israel's apostasy. We see the Spirit as one who altogether exceeds creaturely capacities without destroying them, perfecting them instead. Blessed immortality's principle is the gracious gift of the Spirit, who conforms us to Christ, our only hope. It is the Spirit who, moreover, fills the faithful with the Word's promise, a promise that triumphs over apostasy, using apostasy as the means by which to create an end that exceeds the beginning—God dwelling with and in us as our "timespace."[77] What could be better than that? For with the Lord, there is no corruption.

From here, we move as it were to the horizontal, to the moral, indeed the imperative. How ought we to live, what kind of persons must we be in light of what Peter has proclaimed to us about God's mercy, Christ's grace, and the Spirit's hope? How does the indicative impact and shape the imperative?

Part II

Paul and the Moral Dimension

4

The Invocation of God

We now enter the second section of our treatment, thinking with Paul about the moral and horizontal dimension of his proclamation of the faith. This is not to suggest for a moment that God is irrelevant. No. But it is to suggest that our focus is on the instruction provided for us in regard to life in relation to God. Following Calvin's account of the latter three points constituting the "sum total of Christianity," I have written further chapters on the invocation of God and the fear of God and one rather large chapter on other principal points of heavenly teaching, wherein I treat three key points of heavenly teaching that exemplify both Peter's and Paul's speeches. The points are the resurrection, the pouring out of the Spirit, and the church. These points warrant extended systematic treatment.

Regarding invocation of God, the riches contained in Paul's famous speech to the Athenians in the Areopagus in Acts 17:16–34 are unmatched and unrivaled by any other speeches. There lies therein a wealth of insights both metaphysical and moral. Calvin's comments on the passage help us to see how generously the created order shares with us knowledge of its Creator, encouraging us to call upon him. All living things share in the life of their Creator and declare their participation in him. If we are to unfold well what Calvin calls "the invocation of God," let us be led by the hand

of this God who shows "no partiality," and who teaches Gentiles
and Jews alike to reach out to him as their Maker (10:34).[1]

Before the Athenians

The God whom we invoke is uncreated; he is Maker and not made,
neither identified with nor disengaged from the world he creates
ex nihilo. What God makes is revelatory as it were of himself, having being and agency in relation to himself. Paul's speech teaches
us that the created order is unintelligible in relation to itself. Created things naturally sing a song of praise: "It is he that made us"
(Ps 100:3). This song is their very principle of intelligibility. We
neither author nor preserve ourselves.

Even more astonishing, the maker of the world has a name,
and it is "Lord" (Acts 17:24). This is God's name, YHWH; the Creator is "Lord of heaven and earth." The maker of the world—of
heaven and earth—names himself as one who is sovereign over
what he has made. That is in part what his name Lord connotes.
The Lord does not invoke what he has made but makes it in such
a way as to invoke himself. What the Lord God makes is open
by nature to him; it is not self-enclosed. Nature, as Calvin notes,
gifts us with profitable knowledge of its maker, who is the Lord.
Nature refers us to God. Nature declares that there exists a God
who makes things and is Lord—Lord as a proper name that indicates sovereignty with respect to what is made. God is by nature
one who invokes no created thing for he is Lord, for he needs
nothing in order to be. Paul tells the Athenians that God makes
things, that God has a name, and that the things that God has
made do not rule over him who makes them. Created things are
conditioned while the Creator is not.

We might be tempted to think that the Maker who is Lord made
things for some gain, but Paul says no—"as though he needed anything" (Acts 17:25). The God whom we invoke does not need invo-
cations. How extraordinary! Invocation impacts us—it changes
us—but not the one invoked, who is changeless. Why then does
this God make things if he is not in need of anything? Does not God

at some level desire worship? This is what the religious Athenians do not appreciate. God does not exist in a symbiotic relationship with them. Proper worship of God assumes this: the worshiper and the one worshiped are not codependent. The nature of God is not incomplete, in need as it were of the service of human hands. God is one who bestows being and agency. God is not in need of being, for God is the plenitude of being itself.

God desires that the things he makes invoke him as their Lord.[2] What we have not yet touched on in this speech—Paul's only recorded speech on his secondary missionary journey—but what Paul then does touch on, is what the Lord God is like. The Lord "gives to all mortals life and breath and all things" (Acts 17:25). This God—the Lord—is life and breath; the Lord gives what he is to what he makes, meaning that what he makes has some resemblance to him and participates, however obliquely and distantly, in him. God gives existence because he is existence; gives life because he is life; communicates breath since he is breath. This gives us a glimpse of what he is. Worshipers of the Lord invoke a Lord who is life and breath. Proper worship, then, recognizes that God exists in a noncompetitive though deeply asymmetrical relationship to what he has made. Created things have life and breath by participation, whereas God has them by nature.

It is regretful, I think, that Calvin remarks that Paul is not engaging "in a subtle way with respect to the secret essence of God."[3] I understand that subtlety is, for Calvin, a pejorative term, synonymous in his mind with sophistry and indeed the efforts of the schoolmen. Paul is, I suspect, telling his Gentile audience precious and subtle truths with respect to God's essence that are as elementary as they are profound. The essence of God is coextensive with life and breath.[4] Paul, who is not supposedly speaking of God's essence, if we follow Calvin, continues to proclaim a great deal about God, again deduced from God's act of making. God has no ancestors unlike the nations that "inhabit the whole earth" (Acts 17:26); God's life is eternal, not allotted by either anyone or anything to a specified duration of time. God is uncircumscribed, having no boundaries as it were, being everywhere. God exists in relation to no other thing, having life and breath in himself, conditioning but not being conditioned.

Proper invocation of God takes its cues, then, first, from God. And what God's works establish is a profound appreciation and reminder—"indeed countless"—of three attributes or names of God, in particular, "power, wisdom, and goodness." The God invoked is extravagant in his generosity, leaving boundless and perspicuous "hints of His glory in the handiwork of the world." The world is not a petty and pathetic reminder of his power, wisdom, and goodness, for "plain marks [are] everywhere," argues Calvin.[5] This tells us that God does not discourage invocation but actually encourages our invoking of him. We receive his handiwork as the means by which we grasp something of what the one we are invoking is like. Indeed, God is accommodated to our weakness in such a way that he knows we need "countless"—and not occasional—reminders of his power, wisdom, and goodness. This indicates something about us too, namely that we, Calvin notes, "are not only blind but stupid" because we do not receive "such very clear proofs" in a way that benefits us.[6] We do not receive proofs as a spur to search and seek. Proofs, rightly received, encourage the "search for God" (Acts 17:27); proofs, wrongly received, evoke sloth and indifference in relation to God as if the world were independent of God's being and agency. Remarkably, what one discovers when they search is that God is not actually far away from us. We actually live in him—whether we realize it or not. God is, in fact, so generous that when we search for and invoke him, we "feel his power" as one who is nearer to us than we are to ourselves.[7]

Invocation is the fruit of mindfulness of God. God is so responsive to our groping that when we "pay attention," however shabbily, we "will find Him [God] in himself [ourselves]."[8] That, too, is a striking comment from Calvin regarding what God is like. The God who does not need anything is nonetheless near—as sovereign and transcendent, powerful, wise, and good—those who invoke him, and not only that, but intimate to and indeed in them. Invocation involves paying "attention" to "very clear proofs" so as to "benefit from them" and "feel the presence of God."[9] Is this then to say that "nature alone" is enough? Calvin clearly thinks that nature is transparent to its maker, teaching and indicating God's nature. That said, "with nature alone as our guide our minds cannot penetrate to Him (*illuc*)."[10] We need more than what nature supplies.

The problem, however, is not with nature but rather with the dullness of our minds as evidenced in response to nature. The challenge with respect to proper invocation has to do with the state of our minds. "We ought not to think," proclaims Paul, that our minds are above confusing deity with created things (Acts 17:29). Minds are susceptible and vulnerable to ignorance, to a lack of attention to the createdness of things. This, despite our metaphysical status as made, makes us stupid—"our stupidity is like a monster." We are intellectually and also affectively compromised—"because while feeling Him we do not feel Him." We are made so as to think and feel properly with respect to God. We do not—at least very often and not well—feel God, and so we become stupid. But we do not cease to be made. God preserves us even in our stupidity while not condoning it. We do not cease to be "above all other creatures" because we are and remain, however stupid we may be, "a proof of the glory of God, full of countless miracles as he [the human being] is."[11] The human is proof, argues Calvin, of God's glory; the human is a miracle, full of "created effects without sufficient created causes for them."[12]

The God whom we are to invoke is glorious, and his glory is proved in what he makes, however much the human debases herself. What Paul supplies us with, as he considers the history of Gentile worship of an "unknown," is a surprisingly positive and conciliatory assessment. It is much like Peter's assessment of his own people's apostate history in Acts 3:17. Paul too says that Gentile worship, such as it is, reflects a "time of ignorance." The history of the Jews receives the same apostolic judgment as that of the Gentiles—that is, it too denotes a history of "ignorance." And what proper invocation combats is "times of human ignorance" (17:30). The antidote to ignorance is the basis of invocation, namely God's command to repent.

The Father is the source of all things, the Son the mediator, and the Spirit the preserver. Accordingly, I think it peculiar that Calvin, following the order of Acts 17:28, thinks that life, because it is first in Paul's thinking, is superior to "being." Calvin writes that being is "an inferior thing to both of them [life and movement]." I say peculiar because Calvin's instincts are on this point not so helpful. Let me explain. Calvin argues that knowledge of God is the key to self-knowledge. I concur. Though Calvin makes a promising start by saying "they [Gentiles] have God present in not only the extraordinary gifts of their mind, but in their very being." What Calvin says thereafter is less than helpful. This is, I would argue, because our being is present in God, for our being is, in the mode of likeness, participated being, whereas God is being itself. This is an important point that Calvin does not appreciate. As Calvin rightly says, "Existence belongs only to God, all other things subsist in Him."[13] Existence belongs to God; God possesses it as it were, for existence is coextensive with him, God being existence itself. I think Thomistic metaphysics is helpful at this juncture because it adheres to a more scripturally salient pattern. It is *in* God that we have our being, and therefore our being is a participation via likeness in being itself. When Calvin says that those who know God know themselves as those in whom God is present "in their very being," while not exactly false, it does represent a line of thinking that is not entirely helpful. Our being is a participation in God, whereas God's being is not participated. God is not included in something larger than himself called being. Calvin of course would concur with me on this point, but Calvin's sense that being is inferior to first life and second movement lacks rigor in terms of understanding how creatures are participations in being itself. Indeed, Calvin's caustic comment in this context regarding Pseudo Dionysius' *The Divine Names* as containing "certain things that must not be absolutely despised" is unnecessary given that

Dionysius is, in my view, more of an ally to Calvin than an enemy. Dionysius, too, accounts for the structure of creatureliness in relation to God, though not along lines with which Calvin resonates.

That said, nature is incapable of disclosing truths inaccessible to us. Nature does not declare news of eschatological judgment and the most befitting response to forthcoming judgment, repentance. The God in relation to whom we repent, and whom we invoke, decrees judgment and has "the world judged in righteousness by a man whom he has appointed," Jesus Christ (Acts 17:31). This event and the person at the heart of it are inaccessible to reason and indeed to nature, more broadly. Nature does not proclaim God's judgment of the world in righteousness, but, as we have seen, it does declare its Creator. The natural order does not proclaim God's judgment of the world in righteousness, but nature is not thereby to be despised; even human nature, Calvin notes, is "imbued . . . with some knowledge of God."[14] This knowledge, he continues, is a source from which "true principles" are drawn. If our invocation of God drew only from nature, our invocation of God would be rather incomplete, invoking God as Creator but not also as judge. In terms of the former, we would know that God is our maker and we his offspring, but we would have only a vague and partial sense of the form of life correspondent to our createdness, a life of repentance in light of eschatological judgment in Christ. We would not know that God wants us to repent because of impending judgment.

If God "will have the world judged by a man whom he has appointed," does not that and the command to repent overturn or at least diminish the rather sunny assessment Paul provides and Calvin, also following Paul, offers regarding God present "in their very being" (Acts 17:31)?[15] If we are made to search and grope for the one who "is not far from each one of us," then why is judgment introduced when, as the pagan poets cited recognized, "we are God's offspring" and as such live in God (17:28)? The key to answering these questions is "righteousness" (17:31). Righteousness, too, is coextensive with God. God has and is righteousness. And this is something that in the garden was true of us too, for we walked in harmony with the Lord God, holy and righteous as it were. It was then natural to us to imitate God in righteousness, holiness, and purity. Righteousness, however, is an attribute of God about which pagan philosophers are silent, for those philosophers, at least in times of Paul's citation of them, do not say anything about what God requires of us. They neither explore nor consider a teaching so uncomfortable and strange as divine judgment in righteousness in the risen man Jesus. This is not their fault, for such news involves revelation. Nature speaks primarily of God's relationship to us but only, secondarily, of what that relationship demands of us, namely, that we repent in anticipation of judgment in righteousness, by Jesus Christ. Knowledge of the one who judges in righteousness is (again) inaccessible to them; this news must be proclaimed to them—"when they heard" (17:32).

How does this further fill out our account of invocation? I think it helps us to see how invocation is treated in apostolic preaching in close connection to creation and God's judgment. We are made for righteousness, for imitation of and participation in the one holy God of Israel, the same God who will one day come in Jesus Christ to judge the living and the dead. Some might ask, why on earth does Paul not directly preach the gospel to his hearers and then command them to repent? Why does Paul speak to these Gentiles of God's presence in what he has made, when Paul could 'cut to the chase' by talking to them about the words and deeds of Jesus, and the climax of his preaching and miracles on the cross? Why does Paul tell them to repent without speaking first of Jesus' life, ministry, passion, and death? Why does he fast forward as it were from the structure of creaturely being to eschatological judgment? And why does he discuss Jesus as the one by whom God judges rather than as the judge himself? Does not Paul offer a rather thin gospel to these Gentiles? Really, Paul—do you expect us to repent because God will judge in righteousness by a risen man? Could we not be more general and indeed considerate of where these ignorant Gentiles are at? Why, we might ask, does Paul communicate such a (seemingly) reductive picture? Furthermore, given that Paul focuses on God as Creator and judge and says of Jesus that he is the one by whom God judges, we might even ask why God must judge by this man? Why cannot God judge by himself rather than by appointing another? We might also raise the question as to why resurrection is in the service of judgment in this way?

While it is neither possible nor appropriate to answer all these questions, it is fitting to consider their overall salience regarding invocation. The God we invoke is our Creator and our judge. God gives us, as our Creator and judge, his name, Lord, and he does these things (create and judge) not because he is in need of anything as the Lord but because he is righteousness, perfect goodness and purity. And it is right for the Lord to create offspring, children who live in relationship to him as his offspring. The reason God appoints a risen man to judge is that we might be renewed—indeed remade—in accord with what we are, God's offspring; and the form this becoming takes with respect to all people, Jews and Gentiles, is repentance. This antidote to idolatry and to thinking that we offer God a service is invoking God in the form of repentance. Repentance is both intellectual and moral: intellectual insofar as we abscond from the assumption that God is not sovereign with respect to and independent of what he has made; moral inasmuch as that conflation encourages us to live unrighteously as if there were no one to whom we will give account. Moreover, the overturning and inverting of the Creator/creature relationship make it inconceivable to think the Maker could appoint a resurrected man. Here, our mind, imbued as it is with only general knowledge of God, needs serious perfecting. The form of that perfection is repentance. In repenting before God, we begin to appreciate something of the terrifying grandeur of our Creator God.

The Example to Ephesus

Paul's only recorded speech on his third missionary journey—that is, his speech in Acts 20:18–35 to the Ephesian elders—further enlarges our account of invocation. We saw in my treatment of 17:22–31 something of the theological riches to be gleaned from

Paul's reflection on Athenian invocation of God. We will see in a moment that there is much to be learned about invocation in Paul's speech to the elders, especially as it touches upon Paul's own (cruciform) form of life. Paul's own way of being functions, in his speech, in such a way as to encourage others to invoke God. Paul's speech is bookended by appeals to his own form of life among them—"you yourselves know" (20:18) and "I have given you an example" (20:35). By speaking this way, Paul aligns himself with the grain of the universe. All creatures great and small fulfill their reason for being by testifying in a way appropriate to the kind of creature they are, to their Creator. In the case of humans, we would also want to hold that their Creator is their judge. Paul, as an apostle, points to his way of being, and says to the elders that there is nothing contradictory in terms of his way of being and the one who creates, sustains, and ultimately judges that being in the first place. There is a godly convergence between Paul and the Lord he serves. He invokes his own form of life so that others too may invoke the Lord.

More specifically, Paul invokes his own "humility" and "tears" (Acts 20:19), his not shirking "from doing anything helpful" (20:20), his "endurance" in relationship to "the plots of the Jews" (20:20). Extraordinarily, Paul says that "he does not count [his] life of any value to [him]self" (20:24). Paul's generous reference to his own form of life serves a twofold purpose. First, it aligns with his commendation of the message of God's grace—see 20:24, 32—to them without reservation and, second, that "the weak" be supported (20:35). Who are the weak?

The answer to this question is twofold as well. In one respect, it is all of us. Every one of us needs to be obtained "with the blood of his own Son" (Acts 20:28).[16] Jews and Gentiles alike are in need of cleansing and pardon. But there is more: materially speaking, some are in need of financial support. Paul works in such a way that there is continuity between his own work with his own hands, the message itself, and those who are in need of support. Paul proclaims the message for free so as to be free of the charge that it is his own ambition and need that causes him to proclaim the gospel, rather than Jesus' commandment. Invocation of his own apostolic form of life brings glory to Christ and promotes attention to God's command. Calvin puts it so well when he states that Paul's hope is to be "a faithful and frank interpreter of God."[17] In order for that to happen, Paul's form of life must be commensurate with the God whom he interprets.

"The whole purpose of God" that Paul declares requires a form of life that gives rather than receives. Paul's commendation of a form of apostolic life transparent "to the good news of God's grace" means, over and against Calvin, that "faith toward the Lord Jesus" does not, as Calvin maintains, make "God friendly to us" (Acts 20:21).[18] I understand Calvin's basic point, namely, that God is displeased with Jews and Greeks who remain unrepentant in the face of the good news. That said, faith or the lack thereof does not have the impact upon God that Calvin thinks it does. Whether it be "repentance toward God" or almsgiving, God does not enjoin these upon us so that God may see afresh with respect to us. Instead, God commands us to repent so that we may be made friendly to him. In other words, I am uneasy about Calvin's language for it seems to distort the structure of the Creator/creature relationship. Yes, God is pleased with some Christians while displeased with others, for example, Christians who lack generosity. It is better to say that God always remains friendly toward us, though sometimes we experience God's displeasure when we disobey.

Invocation benefits and changes us as we embrace a form of life that supports the weak; we feel a greater rather than lesser degree of harmony between us and God. The reason that some from the Ephesians' own group will distort the message and savage the flock is because they resist the form of life Paul commends. Indeed, they shirk the cross. They turn away from what Calvin calls "the contemptible form of the cross."[19] Ministers of the gospel will oversee in vain unless their life conforms to the pattern of the one in whose name they oversee. As

Calvin comments, to proclaim the kingdom in a manner befitting God means self-denial, "mortification of our flesh," and "meditation on heavenly life."[20] Insofar as our life is marked in this way, we are blameless, avoiding thereby putting stumbling blocks before others.

The apostolic message "turns the world upside down" (Acts 17:6). This is, in part, because of the form of life that accompanies it (17:6). The apostles may not rule out imprisonment and persecutions. Prayer, self-support (in terms of the apostles), tears, a longing to see the Lord Jesus—this Paul commends so as to encourage (and not discourage) invocation of God, seeing and hearing of the message of God's grace in all its glory. Successful apostolic ministry ends with the people, the elders, on their knees praying; for this the apostles endure imprisonment and persecutions. The apostles live so as to see others praise God, giving thanks to Jesus Christ. The stimulus to a prayerful life is the message of grace. That message assumes even greater power when those who proclaim it are "captive to the Spirit," willing as it were to die for the message (20:22). The message generates such experience.

And so, the speech to the Ephesian elders, ending as it does in prayerful tears, helps us to glimpse a crucial dimension of invocation. Invocation of God evokes a form of life that is exemplary. This is so as not to put stumbling blocks before others' invocation of God, whether they be Jews or Gentiles. The believing "community" that Paul's whole mission achieves in Ephesus yields significant insights regarding invocation.[21] As if that were not enough, we receive further expansion of invocation in another extraordinary speech in which the audience is not simply those Jews virulently opposed to "this Way" but also the Roman tribune (Acts 22:4). With this speech of Paul's, the theocentrism that pervades the other speeches continues, and in a similar vein. We hear Paul describe his conversion—if that is the right word—to Jesus, but it is the tribune Ananias' instruction to Paul that bears fruit for further expansion of our account of invocation.

Before we go there, however, we pause for a moment to consider how Paul's invocation of his own form of life before the Ephesians relates to Sonderegger's proposal, specifically what she deems the "ethical." The "ethical" is of course related to God, the supreme principle of Sonderegger's realism, the God who is there and makes his presence felt.[22] In more explicitly theological terms, "the Processions, that is, are *ethical* properties and relations within the Reality of God."[23] Similarly, she writes, "The Processional Life of God [is to be understood] as *ethical*."[24] What she means is that God's life, the "cauterizing fire" that is God, is, above all, holy.[25] Holiness is the supremely ethical category for God's processional life. "Ethical categories," in other words, are intrinsic to God. I am not sure about this. A more promising way of thinking about the ethical in relationship to God is along that of exemplary lines. What is said of God "substance-wise" is exemplary for human nature. What is said of God "substance-wise" builds upon our nature, giving it a quality that does "not otherwise belong to it by nature."[26] Again, we must be careful here. Paul, for example, encourages his (Gentile) audience to turn from idols to the living God. God is exemplary of life, and the gift of God in Jesus Christ is eternal life. And yet, it does not destroy the life of the creature. It involves, instead, the perfection of that life in the form of life everlasting. It is God's "Nature and Perfections" that are communicated, declared, and imputed to us in Christ, Christ who is our righteousness and sanctification. What is not communicated is "His Persons and Processions." Sonderegger rightly desires to speak of God as an ethical reality. But, in speaking God "twice over," in God's "Nature and Perfections" and then again in "His Persons and Procession," it is the "Processional Life" that is described as ethical.[27] Again, I am not sure about this. It makes more scriptural sense to argue that "His Nature and Perfections" are ethical. Nature talk and perfection talk are "substance-wise" talk. Here, too, however, we must be careful. We distinguish between how, for example, infinity and immutability are modes, not predicates, and not properties.

The one God's mode of being is neither communicable nor imitable. We neither receive by grace absolute infinity nor strive to imitate such in this life. But we do share in divine goodness, for example, in a manner that is relatively infinite. And yet, even in that sharing, that similarity between divine and human, there exists, following Erich Przywara's lead, "the ever-greater dissimilarity."[28] Even so, the participation of the creature (by the grace of Christ) in his Creator is a movement in one direction: from God to us through Jesus. As Davison notes, "Whatever anyone has, he or she has received."[29]

An exemplary form of life is anchored in the primal exemplar, the "Nature and Perfections" of the one God. It is appropriate to speak, then, as does Sonderegger, of the one God as an ethical reality. Where I think it necessary to modify her thinking, is in terms of connecting ethics with God as the exemplar. The revealed law of God—as encapsulated in the Ten Commandments—intensifies and dramatically expounds natural law. Both forms of law participate in their exemplar, God's own nature, albeit in a different way, the former more overtly, the latter less so.[30] Ethics' motor is the attributes common to the one essence of the one God.

Paul's form of life is consistent with his message. You could say that his life participates in it. The form of life commanded by the gospel is consistent with the Lord and Giver of the good news. The issue is one of proper ordering. A life consistent with the gospel is consistent with God, God's nature and perfections. It shares in God through imitation of God's nature and perfections. Sonderegger—as with Barth—so emphasizes the difference between God and creatures that the compatibilism she espies deprives the creature of a meaningful participation in the good that is God. With Sonderegger, it is about God indwelling what is not God, whereas I am championing something of the reverse: the creature participating in God's own nature, embracing habits that encourage virtues resulting in an ever-increasing likeness to God. Divine unicity takes priority here.

Before the Pagan Rulers

Invocation begins with God and receives its creaturely correlate in repentance before God. Paul, as he tells his audience in Acts 22:3–21 about how Jesus met him, speaks of how repentance issues in a life transparent to God. "Who are you, Lord?" (22:8) and "What am I to do, Lord?" (22:10). Jesus gives Saul a new name (Paul) and tells Paul where to go, Damascus. What Paul in due course hears, as he (Paul) follows Jesus' command to go to Damascus, is a word from God spoken by Ananias, "a devout man according to the law" (22:12). Jesus in effect orders Paul to go to Damascus to hear a word from God. "The God of our ancestors" is the God from whom Paul, "a Jew, born in Tarsus in Cilicia," must hear (22:14, 3). What Paul discovers, he reports, and it is that his zeal for God was without knowledge of "his will" (22:14). Paul learns accordingly to invoke God according to God's will and not Paul's zeal. Paul's life offers us an extraordinary contrast between invoking God according to ancestral law (as he receives it) and a christologically charged vision of invocation.[31] The juxtaposition is between "ancestral law" and Paul's lack of knowledge of God's will (22:3). Jesus thinks that Moses wrote about him—Jesus—but Paul has hitherto been unable to see and hear "the Righteous One['s]" voice in Moses' law (22:14). God chooses, so recounts Paul, that he (Paul) sees and hears Jesus in this unambiguously direct way, namely, as blinding light. Paul is not chosen to see and hear through apostolic proclamation of how Moses attests Christ.[32] Instead, Paul is to be a witness (before Jews and especially Gentiles) of the Christ who met him in "a great light" (22:6). Paul sees and hears Christ not, then, through the 'normal' route—apostolic preaching of Christ beginning with Moses—but through direct confrontation, a theophany of sorts (22:6).

Invocation of God begins with God, and God's will, specifically *knowledge* of God's will. And what does God will? Seeing and hearing of Jesus' voice. And what is the result of such? The result is "witness to all the world," meaning not just to the synagogue but to the Gentile world (Acts 22:15). Put differently, invocation of God assumes knowledge of God's will, and what does God will but that people see and hear Jesus resulting in witness "to all the world." In short, invocation involves knowledge of God's will. This is coextensive with seeing and hearing Jesus, and what this seeing and hearing effects is witness.

Paul is tempted to delay invoking the Lord because he cannot quite accept that Israel's God is seen and heard in Jesus. "And now why do you delay?" (Acts 22:16). Seek baptism, and experience your sins being washed away. Paul does so and returns to Jerusalem, wherein, while praying, he sees Jesus saying, "get out" and go "far away to the Gentiles" (22:18, 21). As Jennings writes, "God wants the Gentiles." God seeks to draw "Gentiles into the body of Jesus and into one Spirit with Israel."[33] The means by which God gets hold of the Gentiles is Paul. If Paul is to be the means for such getting hold of, then Paul must invoke God in accord with God's will.

Paul's narration of his testimony in this speech to the tribune (though before a Jewish audience) forces a decision of sorts. As soon as "the brothers and fathers" hear about the Gentile mission, their decision in response to it is revolt (Acts 22:1 and 22:22). One who talks about God in this way, they say, is no Jew. Judaism rejects Paul, full stop. Paul's presentation of Judaism is false, they say; Paul's obedience is not directed toward God. Paul was hearing not God's voice but some other voice. Herein lies the controversy. Is God's will seen and heard in Jesus? Is he Israel's Messiah and the means by which Gentiles are grafted into the covenant made with the ancestors? Or is Jesus someone else and for some other purpose?

There is nothing Paul did that could prepare him to hear and see his ancestral God in the way he did. And yet Paul did see and hear, and what God commands him to do, having been cleansed through the waters of baptism, is call on his name. "Get up," says Ananias, and call on his name (Acts 22:16). And what happens in the first instance of calling on God's name in the temple is that Jesus speaks into a trance elicited by fear of Paul's bearing testimony to Jesus. In words quite tender, Jesus hears Paul's confession of his past persecutions, and, while not commenting on that, Jesus simply says to Paul, "Go" (22:21). We see how calling on God's name, Jesus' name, the name of the Lord—we need not be fussy about consistency—is not a matter of calling upon indifferent ears. As Calvin says, "Invocation of the name of Christ includes in itself the Father and the Spirit."[34] Invocation of Jesus—that, I think, is the reference of "his name"—is a gift of the Father and Spirit, too (22:16). The one God indeed delights in being called upon according to his will. The gift of calling, of invoking, is not only a gift that cleanses but also a gift that sets the believer up for intimacy with God, Father, Son, and Spirit. Again, Calvin: "God allows His saints to unburden their feelings on His bosom in an intimate way."[35] Jesus responds to Paul's unburdening calling by telling him to go. Here Paul, I think, learns a key lesson that will anchor his ministry to the Gentiles. Prayer (calling upon God) is "the best preparation for hearing the voice of God." The blessed voice of the whole and undivided Trinity.[36] Though this is never a domesticated voice, God's presence and command always accompany those obedient to his call.

Just so, it will be the invocation of God that will serve as Paul's strength in his ministry, giving him courage to remind the "brothers and fathers" that he (Paul) has not abandoned the law. Indeed, the foundation of Paul's "witness to all the world" will be a winsome combination of seeing and hearing, beautifully captured by the NRSV's turn of phrase describing Paul's trance in the temple— "saw Jesus saying" (Acts 22:18). Paul enjoys, in the earliest days of his nascent ministry, the vision of Jesus, and it is a vision not of a mute Jesus but instead of a loquacious one. What is a longing for so many, one not normally granted until the life of the world to come, is, for Paul, a present-tense reality as he faces the unsettling truth that mainstream Israel—the synagogue—is not prepared to accept the testimony of one who formerly approved of Stephen's killing. What will sustain Paul in the midst of great opposition is the vision of an eloquent and resplendent Jesus. Paul experiences heaven while on earth. Heaven is present to Saul (Paul) as he dies daily. As Calvin writes, "It is well known that the greatest longing that all the holy had was to be allowed to enjoy the sight of Christ."[37] Paul enjoys that sight now. Invocation rests upon this longing. A precious few in this life are, in the art of invoking itself, granted a vision—"saw Jesus saying"—that for the vast majority of the faithful is reserved for the life of the world to come (22:18).

Invocation and Testimony

The last major point that Paul's two final speeches, both before named Roman magistrates, illuminate, is the relationship between invocation and testimony. We begin with Calvin's keen insight. Commenting on Paul's speech before King Agrippa in Acts 26:2–23, Calvin writes that "we have said elsewhere that *testifying* is more than teaching, for it is as if a solemn contestation were taking place between God and men, to establish the majesty of the Gospel."[38] Invocation is the foundation of testimony (and teaching), and what Paul does before Felix and Agrippa is bear testimony to the gospel's majesty. Invocation relates, as we have seen all along, to God. God is invocation's foundation; testimony, I shall argue, is one of invocation's main fruits. When we consider Paul's speech to Felix (the governor), Paul, not surprisingly, begins with God and thereafter commends a form of life. "But this I admit to you, that according to the Way, which they [the Jews] call a sect, I worship the God of our ancestors, believing everything laid down according to the law or written in the prophets" (24:14). This is a fascinating confession of Paul's self-understanding with respect to the message he is preaching. One might think that Paul would have said: "I worship the God of our ancestors according to the Way." Instead, we have the reverse: "according to the Way . . . I worship the God of our ancestors" (24:14). Paul's description of the object of his worship—"the God of our ancestors"—is expanded, seriously so, by the qualification "according to the Way." I invoke and worship according to the way, the way of this God. Although Jesus Christ is not even mentioned in this speech—though he is in the speech to King Agrippa—the first thing Paul admits in his testimony is the priority of "the Way." One might immediately think of Jesus' own words in this context in John 14:6: "I am the Way." This is not of course problematic so long as we do not exclude Paul's actual reference. "The Way" has rather more to do with a name given to the community inclusive of Jewish believers in the Messiah Jesus as well as Gentiles—"which they call a sect" (Acts 24:14). Invocation's location is this sect, and its object is worship of "the God of our ancestors" (24:14). "The Way" is both vertical and horizontal in its reference. The Way involves worship of "the God of our ancestors" according to Christ—the vertical. Also, because worship is according to Christ, no dividing wall remains between Jews and Gentiles. This is evidence of the message's horizontal impact. Invocation of God assumes a home—an eschatological community of Jewish and Gentile believers that takes up space—according to Christ as raised and Christ as the center of God's judgment of the righteous and the unrighteous.

What remains noticeable as the speech unfolds is the priority ascribed to God. Paul testifies to Felix that he has "a hope in God—a hope that they themselves accept—that there will be a resurrection of both the righteous and the unrighteous" (Acts 24:15). One might think that the hope in God that Paul has would, as he articulates it before this pagan ruler, have more christological density. Surprisingly, hope's center is not directly identified with the crucified, risen, and ascended Christ. Instead, Paul points to a future resurrection of both the righteous and unrighteous. This seems a bit odd. Why does "faith in Christ Jesus" not feature more prominently as it does, for example, in Paul's conversations with Felix's Jewish wife, Drusilla (24:24)? God is, in the speech to Felix, worshiped, hoped in, and the one before whom Paul's conscience is clear. The register is so strongly theocentric that we cannot but conclude that invocation, properly practiced, is first and foremost toward God as is the case with testimony. When testifying, the thing that Paul thinks most important to notice (before pagans) is not Jesus' resurrection but instead the general resurrection (which of course assumes Jesus' resurrection). That has in Paul's speech priority, but why? And what are some of the implications for invocation?

I think the reason has to do with a perspicuous comment that Calvin makes. Calvin notes that there is "no sharper stimulus to the desire to lead an upright and holy life, than the hope of the final resurrection, as Scripture reminds us in many passages."[39] The final resurrection—the hope thereof—is in both Calvin's mind and Paul's mind the best stimulant for a holy life, a life of faithfully invoking God. The reason that the Jewish nation regards their Messiah as a criminal is because it lacks godliness, expressed, fundamentally, in unbelief. Israel does not fear God, who will judge all on the last day through his Messiah. The eschatological resurrection stimulates a holy life, and a holy life is *the* prerequisite for "according to the Way" worship of the God of our ancestors. Worship and hope assume holiness. The way to worship and to hope involves embrace of an "upright and godly life." What stimulates such hope is a pious life, and a pious life assumes "according to the Way" worship of "the God of our ancestors" (24:14). Invocation is coextensive with a way of life that looks forward in faith to final judgment. Such a life is a godly life, and without such a life, there is little point in talking about "faith in Christ Jesus" (24:24).

When we turn to Paul's last speech before the Roman authorities, his speech to King Agrippa, offered up just before he sails to Rome, we find that the priority and promise of God remain front and center as it were but with a surprising and subtle christological twist. This twist, as it were, provides a fitting conclusion to an account of invocation. Most startling in this speech is Paul's expansion of his conversion narrative. What Paul offers us here is far more fulsome than what he offers to the tribune Felix in Acts 26:2–23. Most significant is the sense that Jesus speaks (far) more than he does in the previous description that Paul offers. Here in 26:2–23 Jesus says to Paul: "for I have appeared to you for this purpose, to appoint you to serve and testify to the things in which you have seen me and to those in which I will appear to you" (26:16). I ask, what are those "things in which you have seen me" (26:16)? The answer is Moses and the prophets. As Calvin notes, the Christian faith flows from "the Jewish religion."[40] It is as if Jesus were saying to Paul, "Testify to my presence in the Law and the Prophets," that there is nothing in the gospel of me that is "in disagreement with, or far removed from, the Law and the Prophets."[41] You have seen me here, says Jesus, though refused to recognize me. And then there is the ambiguous reference to the future: to testify "to those [things] in which I will appear to you" (26:16). The inference is that Jesus will continue to appear to Paul, and that Paul must "serve and testify" accordingly (26:16). Jesus' sermon to Paul in the vision, as Paul recounts it before another pagan ruler, is as simple as it is matchless in its inexhaustible mystery.

Invocation is directed Godward. God is its principle. It is noteworthy that even Jesus' address to Paul, as Paul recounts it, is theocentric in its own way. Paul's ministry to the Gentiles, as one sent by the Lord Jesus, is "to open their eyes so that they may turn from darkness to light and from the power of Satan to God" (26:18). Jesus desires Gentiles to turn to God. Even then, Gentiles do so by faith in Jesus himself. Faith in Jesus is coextensive with turning to God. Faith, as Calvin notes, "is the one and only foundation of piety"; faith in Jesus is the object, and the *telos* of faith in Jesus is God.[42] Faith in Jesus is directed Godward, just as is the testimony given by Jesus to Paul—"from darkness to light and from the power of Satan to God" (26:18).

In keeping with this, when Paul unfolds his story as it were to King Agrippa, whom he (Paul) is persuading to become a Christian via "the prophets," it is God who is preeminent—if that is indeed the right word! Consider the way in which Paul invokes God before the King: "the promise made by God to our ancestors" (Acts 26:6). This is the God for whom it is *not* incredible that the dead are raised, the God to whom the Gentiles would turn, and the God who helps Paul in testifying to the prophets and Moses (26:27, 6). God is the absolute foundation for Paul's being sent to the Gentiles, God too with respect to Jesus of Nazareth's rising from the dead in whom we are to have the sanctification of faith. When Paul prays "to God that not only you [Agrippa] but also all who are listening to me today might become such as I am," we see (again) the pattern of invocation. Its foundation and end are God. But God would have us become Christians that we "may receive forgiveness of sins and a place among those who are sanctified by faith in me" (26:18). Jesus does not turn us to himself but to Moses and the prophets in order that we might turn from "darkness to light and from the power of Satan to God" (26:18). In turning from them, we turn to God, and thus invoke him according to his Son, bearing Spirit-filled testimony to him in life and in death.

Conclusion

To conclude this chapter on invocation, it is fitting to refer to Paul's last and briefest speech to the Jewish leaders in Rome. Invocation has (once again) to do with God. Invocation is the basis for "testifying to the Kingdom of God" and "proclaiming the Kingdom of God" (Acts 28:23, 31). "The people of Israel" are to invoke God, and, to invoke God rightly, Israel must do the opposite of what "your ancestors" have done, as spoken of by the prophet Isaiah. What the ancestors have not done, and what must be done, is "listen," which is what Paul knows the Gentiles will do (28:28). Listening, however, is no panacea. Isaiah of course says that people may listen "but never understand," and "look, but never perceive" (28:26). If we are to invoke the God whom Paul proclaims and testifies in such a way that listening will be coextensive with understanding, looking with perceiving, then we must call upon God, who promises to heal—"and I would heal them" (28:27). Invocation assumes a pedagogy, that is, learning to see Jesus in "the law of Moses" and "the prophets" in order to receive God's salvation (28:23). Without calling upon God as he meets us in the law and prophets as fulfilled in Jesus, then there is every possibility of listening without understanding and looking without perceiving. God wants to heal our hearts, ears, and eyes, but the only way for them to be healed is if we call upon Israel's hope, listening to him as he speaks through Moses and the prophets about Jesus Christ. Of this final speech, Calvin says, "We also learn from this that it is only those who direct their gaze to Christ and His spiritual Kingdom who have the proper hope."[43]

In sum, I have shown in this chapter something of the essence and implications of Paul's speaking regarding invocation. I have emphasized invocation's rootedness in God. I have described how the natural order, the end-time judgment, and Paul's own form of life spur invocation of God. Whether it be before the Athenians, the Ephesian elders, the "brothers and fathers," or pagan rules, invocation is a many-layered theme, immensely generative of the contours of life lived before God according to the Way. At this point, we are ready to say something more about what invocation encourages, namely, the fear of God. Apostolic preaching has done its work insofar as men and women learn to fear the God who lies at its center.

5

The Fear of God

Having thought through something of the nature of our invocation of God, let us think, with Paul, about a close correlate, namely the fear of God. We begin with Paul's first recorded speech to the synagogue in Perga (Acts 13:16–41). This speech is, not surprisingly, fertile ground for contemplation of the fear of God. "You Israelites, and others who fear God, listen" (13:16). Also 13:26: "My brothers, you descendants of Abraham's family, and others who fear God, to us the message of this salvation has been sent." Fear of God, the ground of piety, is not, as we shall note, confined to Israel, Abraham's family, alone. God has created the world in such a way that it is not self-contained. The material order is structured in such a way as to encourage fear of its Creator. What this implies is something of a rough sense, common to all people, of God, of God's terrible magnificence and grandeur, of God as the uncreated ground from which and ceaseless ground to which all things are directed. There have always been women, men, and children who fear God, at every time and in every place. That is not to say that such people are saved; saved is not the right designation, for it assumes the light of revelation, indeed of who saves and what we are saved from. However, this is to say that the message of salvation has two recipients in mind—first, "Israelites," and second, "others who fear God." These others are Gentiles, and their fear instructs us regarding how the world witnesses to God.

Paul offers here a remarkably positive example of how pervasive and deep the sense is, present among all people everywhere and at all times, that God is to be feared. This is, to be sure, a mystery into which we must pray if our minds are to be enlightened. As we pray and listen to Paul, we see that salvation (freedom from sin) does not overturn the fear of God. Instead, the fear of God remains most commendable. Furthermore, if fear of God is present among many and varied, though by no means necessarily all, this demonstrates, I think, the sacramental character of all reality. The creation is at its most basic essentially open to and directed toward its Creator, sharing in his being and agency via likeness. It is a sign. Fear of God aligns with a strong and reverent sense of being made, of being upheld in being by God and superintended toward him. We are made in such a way that openness to God as one to be feared is inscribed in our very humanity. The natural world and conscience encourage fear of God. And yet, that fear does not save; only the salvation sent to us saves, though that fear, as we saw with Cornelius, denotes receptiveness to the Savior.

What then is the divine purpose of this fear that Paul seems to think is especially prevalent among Gentiles? Fear is the abiding foundation of love for God. Love of God does not destroy fear, but love is indeed what perfects it. "There is no fear in love, but perfect love casts out fear," writes John in 1 John 4:18. Even then, fear, as with devotion, is prone to grave error. The Jews—namely, the leadership of the synagogue—incite, upon hearing Paul's preaching, "devout women of high standing" to persecute Paul and Barnabas (Acts 13:50). These men may perceive themselves to be God fearers. However, their actions suggest otherwise. Fear of God may not be conflated with devotion. Instead, genuine fear of God is present when the Messiah is received by faith and honored in love. Fear, in other words, is incomplete. We may fear God, in other words, without repentance that issues in love. This is true of many Jews in Paul's audience in the synagogue at Perga. Hence

Paul's warning to his Jewish hearers: "Beware, therefore, that what the prophets said does not happen to you" (13:40).

Fear is not something that belongs to God. We speak, rightly, of, for example, the goodness of God, for goodness belongs to God and is proper to God himself, but fear is not. Fear is not an attribute, perfection, or name of God. Fear is not said of both God and creatures, analogically speaking, as goodness is. Fear is, instead, a response to the sense of God naturally implanted within us. We fear God because, as all people everywhere recognize, however obliquely, we do not have being in relation to ourselves but in relation to another, namely God. But, as with "the residents of Jerusalem and their leaders," many of us do not recognize what we are, creatures of a God to be feared and who sends his salvation not just to Jews but to Gentiles as well (Acts 13:27).

I agree with Calvin, who argues that election is "antecedent to faith" as is the case with, I think, fear of God.[1] Fear of God and election are antecedent to faith. Fear is fulfilled in faith; fear yields to faith. Belief, though, does not negate fear but instead perfects it in the form of love. Yes, we should, as Paul, indeed in his speech in Athens acknowledges, grant that God "is not far from each one of us" (17:2). Such apprehension evokes fear, but fear is not the end game, for fear is often mixed, as Paul notes, with "the times of human ignorance" (17:30), especially in the case of Gentiles who lack "the covenants" (Rom 9:4). Fear is not the ultimate response God desires from his people. Again, God desires to be not only revered—feared—but worshiped and worshiped in accordance with his promise to "have the world judged in righteousness by a man whom he has appointed" (17:31). Worship that pleases God includes fear but is not to be equated with fear. Fear is incomplete. Israel's horizon is repentance and its *telos* love. Fear is analogous to a help given us by God, a help intrinsic to our natural sense that we are surrounded by God's "glory in the handiwork of the world."[2] But we derive no benefit from fear of God if such fear does not lead to a turning from sin culminating in love for God. Fear of God *may* be a help to us. However, if we only let it help us but not profit us, then we are unable to worship God in a proper and devout way. The fear of God that is "imbued," as Calvin says, in us "by nature" must be perfected by "the voice of the Gospel" as the gospel sounds in our ears, for by that same gospel God "is urging us to repent."[3]

It is critical, moreover, that the referent of the language of fear in Acts, as is the case throughout Scripture, is God (the Father), creator of heaven and earth, of all things visible and invisible. Fear issuing in repentance is directed toward God, God who is present "in their [our] very being."[4] Just so, fear is never directive to Jesus: "faith toward our Lord Jesus" is, instead, what Paul commands, but repentance is (again) directed "toward God" (Acts 20:22). This suggests (again) the preparatory and imperfect character of fear. Fear must indeed be accompanied by repentance and faith. Fear is an accommodated disposition. It, as with the created order in general, has a pedagogical purpose, more befitting of those ignorant of the law and prophets, indeed of the good news of God's grace in the Lord Jesus. Fear acknowledges God the Creator; repentance turns to the Creator God, and "faith is the receiving of grace which is presented to us in Christ."[5] The fear of God must regulate our life, having a kind of broad moral purpose in discouraging vice, but unless Christ meets us, fear of God remains inadequate. Fear is completed when it yields faith in apostolic preaching.

Fear and Beneficence

We have focused on the function of created things in invoking fear, but there is another feature that, although more muted, is nonetheless profoundly important to an account of fear, and that is "beneficence." Calvin writes, "Nothing brings men nearer to God than beneficence."[6] To cast this in salvific terms, while God "begins to save us" by leading us through visible (and created) things to fear of him, "He brings forward His Word as the instrument for salvation."[7] "His Word" refers, in Calvin's mind, to the person of the Lord Jesus but also his words. The words of the Word preserve us in a saving way by holding forth the beneficence by which we are brought near to God. Fear does not bring us near in as direct a way, but faith in the words of the Word, as expressed in beneficence, does. Supporting the weak does more to bring us to God than anything else. Beneficence does not abandon fear but, as with faith, indicates its maturity, for beneficence is other-directed. Fear's direction is more properly vertical. While beginning with the vertical—God as beneficence itself—beneficence is completed in the horizontal; beneficence has a more immediate horizontal dimension.

Nature is not devoid of the presence of the one in whom it exists, on whom it depends, and with whom it enjoys a participating relationship. Nature is graced because it refers, quite naturally, to what is above it. Also, grace, as Calvin writes, "is not tied to the sacraments."[8] Grace comes, for example, through supporting the weak. Such giving graces—blesses—the recipient as well as the one who gives. This is useful to point out, different as it is from fear of God, which is more of a receptive phenomenon. Fear is an appropriate response to nature's testimony and to conscience, while beneficence is far more than receptive. Beneficence is, instead, intrinsic to charity. As Denys Turner notes, "The charity by which we love our neighbor is a sort of participation in the divine charity."[9] That is why it is more blessed to give than to receive. Giving in support of the weak is "precisely where the presence of God's agency is most evidently and directly working."[10] For in acting charitably, in giving to the weak, those who give are participating, freely, in that which is of God and God himself. God works in choices and actions that are participations, however distantly, in what God is. While fear is a fitting response to nature's testimony and, as such, is receptive in nature, beneficence is greater, for it gives the support anchored in charity. Giving is participatory in the giver of all good gifts, God (cf. Jas 1:17).

And so, when it comes to the fear of God, it is clear that it is not the last word as it were. That said, we must take it seriously. Think for a moment about Paul's speech to Felix (Acts 24:16–21) and dimensions there that have recourse to fear of God. Paul's "worship [of] the God of our ancestors" (24:14), Paul's "hope in God"

(24:15), and Paul's "clear conscience toward God and all people" (24:16) assume fear of God, do they not? There is not any worship and hope, for instance, without fear, but we do not worship and hope so as to provoke more fear. In worshiping and hoping with a clear conscience and not less, fear may (again) be perfected. One may in other words fear God but still be largely in darkness. Similarly, one may revere the testimony of the prophets and Moses without hearing testimony of the Messiah therein and of his being the first to rise from the dead. Fear *may* encourage us to "give heed to how God wishes to save," but fear, also, may not.[11] Fear may open eyes "so that they may turn from darkness to light and from the power of Satan to God," but also fear may not. Why? Because fear is a lesser good than faith. The message Jesus gives to Paul has it that faith in Jesus himself sanctifies. Sanctifying faith assumes (again) fear, but fear does not necessarily lead to sanctifying faith. Sanctifying faith has as its agent the Lord Jesus. This is again not to disparage fear, but fear "without Christ and His faith" is indeed "wretched."[12] Fear possesses a salutary sense of God but is impoverished when contrasted with the blessings of faith—for example, "forgiveness of sins" (26:18).

There is, indeed, throughout Scripture the idea that certain responses to God are more praiseworthy than others. Fear, while commendable, is superseded by faith, to say nothing of faith working through love. Nonetheless, without fear, we will only listen and never understand, look but not perceive. As with Moses and the prophets, we cannot receive Jesus without receiving them, but were we to receive them and not receive Jesus, we would not have received them at all. Without fear, there is no faith, but faith, having perfected fear (and never the inverse), aims at love, expressed in beneficence.

Fear and Sight

We see, not surprisingly, complementary insights in Stephen's great speech (Acts 7:1–53). Let us turn back as it were for a moment. One may receive "the law as ordained by angels," as indeed Israel did, but not keep the law. Similarly, we Gentiles may receive nature's and conscience's testimony to its Creator and the moral law but derive no benefit by not worshiping the Creator of all. Receiving may not necessarily be equated with keeping. Fear may not be immediately identified with an inner spirit obedient to God. And even then, as with the rich young ruler in Mark 10:17–31, we may obey without giving to God the love at which the commandments aim. To describe fear as the highest response to God is accordingly wrong. Fear lacks an awareness of the heart of the second article of the Creed; fear lacks the truths of revelation. We may hear and yet be "stiff-necked," for we have not reckoned with the risen Righteous One who is at God's right hand. We may fear God, but we may also resist the direction of the fear of God working in us, impelling us toward the righteous One.

The dynamic is illustrated in Stephen's martyrdom. The righteous One is seen by Stephen, though none of those around him see. Stephen sees what they do not see. We may deduce from this that the "brothers and fathers" (Acts 7:21) whom Stephen addresses do not see. That is because they do not fear God. Had they at least feared their God, they might be a little less opposed to the Holy Spirit, whom Stephen says they "are forever opposing" (7:51). Though elementary as fear may be, they—"brothers and fathers"—might have realized, had they feared God, that "the Most High does not dwell in houses made with human hands" (7:48). But instead, the "brothers and sisters," following the lead of the ancestors, proceed as if God were one of their own, domesticable. Fear—the most elementary sense that God is other, transcendent if you will, though not in a way "that excludes positive fellowship with the world"—births knowledge.[13] This is knowledge of God that, while somewhat rough and unrefined—not yet subject to God's raising of Jesus and the ensuing final judgment—is nevertheless epistemologically significant. The sin of the ancestors and "brothers and fathers" (7:2) prevents them from knowing, let alone seeing, things as they are. What they do not know because of their sin is that Stephen is in love with the same God whom they suppose themselves to, at least, fear. But unlike the "brothers and fathers," Stephen "see[s] things that are there to be seen."[14] Being filled with the Holy Spirit as he is, and so possessing a purity of heart and mind that they do not, Stephen sees that Moses and the prophets speak of Jesus. Stephen bears witness to Jesus in death and, as a result, sees what they cannot see, Jesus himself.

Fear of God sees that things are created. Fear recognizes that there is something—"for from nothing to something is not a trajectory at all"—and that something is because of God. God is "an unutterable mystery at the heart of whatever there is."[15] Were the "brothers and fathers" to have feared such a God, they would have at least been open to accepting the sad truth that their ancestors persecuted every one of the prophets. "Which one of the prophets did your ancestors not persecute?" (Acts 7:51). Because of their sin and concomitant lack of any fear of God, the sad and tragic reality of their own history as Stephen narrates it is unintelligible to them.

Stephen, however, knows what they do not, namely, that even as he speaks the heavens are being opened. The "brothers and fathers" hear Stephen but see nothing. Stephen exemplifies that deep Johannine truth, namely, that "there is no fear in love, but perfect love casts out fear; for fear has to do with punishment, and whoever fears has not reached perfection in love" (1 John 4:18). God is now more intimate to Stephen than Stephen is to himself. Stephen has perfect love. This love reaches toward God and prays for forgiveness for those who have "not reached perfection in love."

At the heart of the fear of God is the elementary acknowledgment of our own mortality and impending death. We are not our own. Instead, we are from, through, and for this God who makes all things, visible and invisible. Heaven is his throne, and earth is his footstool. Heaven is not our throne, and earth is not our footstool. A martyr's death, as is Stephen's, is the fitting perfection of fear, for his fear of God has been completed in love and rewarded with sight. Fear is something of a midwife, then. It is how we begin to see and hear: to hear the prophets bearing the Spirit's voice, to see heaven disclosing Jesus. Stephen's martyrdom is where Peter's preaching of the One whom God raised leads. Hearts filled with the Spirit as is Stephen's lead to the beatific vision; hearts like those of Ananias and Sapphira that lie to the Spirit result in death. In Turner's memorable words, we get "the martyr's death into our bones" when we, with the church's first martyr, see "the Son of Man standing" (Acts 7:56).[16] Then, we may, with Stephen as our model, continually offer over our lives to the Father through Jesus. The fear with which we may have initially greeted Jesus—"Go away from me, Lord, for I am a sinful man!"—evokes our repentance, and that repentance is fulfilled in love (Luke 5:8). As Mascall states of the theologian, though this is of course something that is "the primary need" of all Christians, it is of utmost importance to be "in love with God."[17] Stephen shows us the blessed fruit of that "primary need," sight of God's glory and Jesus standing. Fear is where being in love with God begins. We cannot become like Stephen overnight, but we may begin by, first, getting Jesus' resurrection into our bones through listening to Moses and the prophets declare him. As we do, we "see things that are there to be seen."[18] We see what the young man before whom coats are being laid does not see. We see, indeed, the one who shall soon show himself to Saul in such a way that Saul will no longer see until his sight is restored by Ananias enabling him to see then the one he had tried to destroy.

Put somewhat differently, the natural order naturally evokes fear of God. Fear is the most natural response to the lessons that nature (and conscience) would teach: we are not our own. When such reverent awareness gives way to faith, our status changes for we see the Creator as also our judge. His judgment is to be feared, yes, but he judges through the one whom he has appointed by raising him from the dead. The judge has been judged in our place.[19] We greet his judgment with love, in accordance with our "supernatural status" as Christians.[20] We see that all things are through this one who was raised to judge all peoples, and that he is most warmly received when we tell him, as did Peter, that we love him, even if, as Jesus said of Peter, we must die in a way that we do not want to die (cf. John 21:15–19).

Even then, however, the fear of God, intrinsic as it is to faith, discourages us from producing naturalistic "explanations of the primordial Christian events."[21] The fear of God dissuades us from assuming that the spectacular spread of the gospel throughout Asia Minor in the second half of the first century has nothing to do with God. It is because of God that Paul while under house arrest welcomes all, "proclaiming the Kingdom of God and teaching about the Lord Jesus Christ with all boldness" (Acts 28:20). Our doctrine of God has to allow for the fact that God, in raising Jesus, declares, through his apostolic servants, a gospel that is profoundly attractive. The Gentiles listen as they do because this message—the kingdom of God—contains within itself profound self-authenticating power. Fear of God accordingly serves a key pedagogical purpose: that of never reducing the gospel's spread and subsequent embrace to anyone other than God. Do not, in other words, suggest that the Gentiles' listening has anything other than God as its baseline foundation. We fear God, even as we learn to trust and love God, because of our propensity toward taking what is God's—ultimate responsibility for the gospel's spread—unto our shoulders. No, the gospel's propagation is God's work all the way down, employing us as instruments through whom the good news spreads.

Fear and Confidence

Those among whom the gospel will for the most part take root—the Gentiles—listen, but, as with Israel, unless an Israel-like account of the believing community is operative, then, problems arise. Looking without perceiving cannot, even among predominantly Gentile Christian communities, be dismissed as something descriptive only of the ancestors of Israel. Fear of God as a perpetually relevant Christian disposition has this function. It teaches us to be mindful of the extent to which apostasy lurks in all our hearts, especially among those who perceive themselves to be most intimate to God and God's purposes. When we refuse to fear God, we make Christian faith over into our image, relying on our own preeminence to explain what is of God and our standing with God. Insofar as we do so, our hearts grow dull, and this we cannot allow. And so fear serves as a useful antidote to adultery, and a spur to reinhabit the theocentric character of the promise, namely, that it is God who promises and God who sustains a people in it, fulfilling it by raising his Son and at the end judging all through him.

Paul's arrival in Rome is preceded by his arduous journey there. Paul's journey includes of course his shipwreck. Fear of God constrains Paul on every side, not because the God in whom Paul believes is unstable and untrustworthy, but because God's purposes are secure. Even the obduracy of God's covenant people cannot overcome God's purposes. Accordingly, we are to fear God, though we are to fear him, because with this God things are exactly as told. Fear generates a confidence because there is nothing in God's promise that would dissuade us from thinking that it is our power and glory that, as it were, establishes the promise, let alone fulfills it. In Paul's case, God grants "safety" as God does to all those on the ship simply because God wills that Paul bear testimony in Rome to the emperor (Acts 27:24). Paul is not to fear the prospect of being shipwrecked, but, as is the case with all of us, Paul is to 'fear' his own predilection for reducing what is of God to Paul himself. Yes, the men throw wheat to the sea so as to buoy the ship upward. This they do—they exercise an agency appropriate to God's promise—all the while recognizing, with fear, that God's will that Paul stands before the emperor is unable to be thwarted. Yes, we fear God even as we learn to trust and love him in accord with the gospel. This we do because we know all too well our extraordinary ability to naturalize, taking what is of God and either usurping or claiming it for ourselves. Acts' steady theocentrism keeps the fear of God alive, reminding us that the spread of the message even to Rome is God's doing, God's work, the God who uses the powers and operations of creatures to bring about his purposes.[22] That is the power behind Paul's "boldness" and lack of "hindrance" (28:31). Reflecting on the advance of the kingdom and its reach, we are reflecting on what is of God.

Fear of God is coextensive with Christian faith though not exhaustive of Christian faith. Christian faith's ultimate horizon is the glory of the thrice-holy God. This God achieves preeminence in us when we receive in faith the apostolic testimony to his kingdom and the message of Jesus from Moses and the prophets. Again, the fear of God does not encompass Christian faith. Instead, Christian faith, as we have been learning all along, is a matter of "a lively awareness of the grace of God, which brings genuine joy from the certainty of salvation."[23] Fear of God is not comprehensive of the response to the gospel. What it does mean, however, is that when teaching and preaching the gospel, God matters. This is the God of Moses and the prophets. We therefore ought to fear this God who remains the subject and agent of his gospel, triumphing over all opposition to it.

"Penitence," as Calvin notes, "requires fear."[24] Without fear, it is hard to hate sin and to stand with any degree of integrity before God. No wonder Felix is afraid of Paul's speaking concerning faith in Christ Jesus (cf. Acts 24:25). Felix begins to fear God because the first stirrings of penitence begin to flicker regarding "his disgraceful money making, of his plundering, cruelty, and lax government."[25] Though Felix only wanted money from Paul so as to release Paul, Felix yet converses with Paul because at some level there is something strangely and appealingly befuddling about discussions with Paul. This should not surprise us. The fear of God encourages us to remember that it is God's "property . . . to govern events contrary to what men expect," even the conversation of an apostle with a corrupt Roman prelate.[26] Our expectations are rather fallible. Though Felix is a callous political operator, God's hands are not tied as it were with respect to Felix's shenanigans. Felix, as with all of us, lives within divinely appointed bounds, bounds over which we cannot leap, however hard we may try.

Thus we fear God because we cannot leap over them, resting confidently in God's promise that the good news will be proclaimed to the whole Gentile world. We fear a God who will protect his faithful from the bite of a viper if that "be for the glory of this Gospel."[27] Without a lively fear of God, we take what is of God—God's healing of Paul's snakebite—and use it to construct an idol, in this case, Paul himself as one to be worshiped.[28] The "natives" transfer the glory due to God to a person, namely Paul. They do not fear God and lack the glimmers of faith that perfects it. This is the idolatrous human heart at work: "Men are ungrateful to God and transfer His glory to another person or thing."[29] Without fear, we (again) naturalize the gifts of God. We assume that what is of God is actually of and for ourselves. Again, we follow the example of those original to the island of Malta, assuming that Paul is not killed by the viper because of God but because he (Paul) is a god. Quite the contrary: Paul owes his deliverance to God, full stop. It is this that Paul wants the inhabitants to recognize. Paul is preserved, as he is, because the message of salvation is to reach Rome and, more broadly, the Gentiles.

Fear of God leads to a rejection of idolatry. On the one hand, we can see how fear of God is manifest in rejecting worship of what is not the one God. For Sonderegger, divine oneness is paired with a rejection of idols.[30] It is worthwhile to take a moment to assess the impact of her work on the account of fear sketched thus far. In this sense, divine oneness is ethical. So far, so good. Where I think things are opaque in Sonderegger's proposals is in terms of the doctrine of creation. Metaphysical "compatibilism just is the doctrine of creation," Sonderegger avers.[31] Put differently, the goodness of all is God, yet God is not identical with things, even though God "inhabits, indwells, and irradiates."[32] But why does God create things? That question remains unanswered. The divine will's "dogmatic role," for Sonderegger, is "to preserve the freedom of God's action *ad extra*."[33] Yes, God acts toward what is not God on the basis of his will. His will, however, is one and simple in him. God's will, then, is commensurate with his goodness, and

God's will "is not repugnant to his simplicity."[34] God is good, and therefore God creates things—"all things have been made in order to be likenesses of the divine goodness."[35] The need to secure God's freedom via God's will is obviated when divine goodness is installed at the center. The notion of divine freedom is a distinctly modern one, a way of securing God's difference with respect to what God makes and sustains. While that is of course laudable, what really encourages fear of God is not so much that God is free with respect to what God makes but that God makes things "in order to be likenesses of the divine goodness."[36] God so delights in the good God is—there could be nothing better than being created in the manner of a likeness of a good God. Accordingly, we fear God because we are not God but, instead, likenesses of one who needs nothing in order to be. The compatibility between Creator and creature—that God wills a world to be that is open to himself—is secured, then, in Sonderegger's mind by the communicable attributes. God is present to creatures, communicating thereby himself—his divine nature—to them. We must, if we are to follow Sonderegger's lead, derive the reasons for their being anything at all only retrospectively. There is something because God's perfection is "Communicable Perfection."[37] Things are, and know themselves to be created, because God indwells them. This is, for Sonderegger, the basis of creaturely fear of God. I do not think this is adequate.

An understanding of Creator and creature that is more participatory grounds fear directly in divine aseity. The God we fear is one who is the likeness of no thing. God just is, and created things are because God is good. What secures the "freedom" of God in relation to what is not God, then, is the divine nature itself. God's acts are free because God is good—"since the active thing does everything that it does on that account."[38] God is to be feared because God is good. God loves what God is—goodness itself—by virtue of God's will. The freedom of God's activity in relationship to what is not God assumes a thick account of simplicity. In Thomas' terms, God "understands himself, the perfect good. . . . But one necessarily loves the understood good and does so by the will."[39] To say this differently, God acts according to his essence, which includes his will. For Sonderegger, God's acts are according to "His Nature and Person." For Thomas, God *acts* according to; for Sonderegger, God's acts are "His Nature."[40] Herein lies the difference between Thomas and Sonderegger. Accordingly, I think it is more fitting to articulate an emphasis different from Sonderegger's and more in line with Thomas'. For Sonderegger, the emphasis is on our "dear LORD's Humble Presence in all existents,"[41] whereas I emphasize the presence of all likenesses (existents) in the Lord. Because creation and providence are integrated doctrines, themselves downstream of the doctrine of God, God's relations to creatures are not so much of a form of "a Transcendental Presence."[42] Instead, God's relations toward creatures assume a participatory structure. God creates likenesses, and likenesses are open to and refer back and toward the one whose likenesses they are. The God we fear does not admix his "own Being and Light with our small light."[43] No, our lights, such as they are, share in his, yes, as likenesses. The relation of creatures to God is real, but God's relations with us are not. This is not to suggest that Sonderegger thinks God gains something from being in relationship to us—far from it! And yet, the language of admixing is curious, nonetheless. God acts savingly in relationship to us in the mission of the Son and Spirit in order that we, as his likenesses, might be restored to genuine likenesses. The God we fear in life and in death does not so much live "*in* the concrete."[44] Instead, the concrete lives in him as a likeness. God is the kind of God who extends goodness to creatures in such a way that no matter how hard they try to untether themselves from him, the very structure of their being ensures that they will never ultimately succeed. Whatever stage in which we may find ourselves, in this life, we cannot cease to be those whose life is not their own. Yes, as Williams states, we live "the divine life in the mode of reception and response."[45] But that reception and response assume a basic participation—by nature—in the one to whom we respond. If such is the case, then, we thereby also avoid the problematic nature of the language of paradox to describe the relation of Creator/creature. Let me explain.

Williams introduces the notion of paradox in order to illuminate "analogical understanding," as he calls it.[46] One of the curious dimensions of Williams' presentation of "analogical understanding" is that the idiom is one of "agency" and not that of being.[47] I do not know why this is. Williams' main point is that Christ's humanity—its "*esse*"—"contributes nothing extra to that identifying *esse*." As with Sonderegger, the Word's existence is not conflated with the human *esse* or subsumed by it. The being of Jesus' humanity does not contribute anything to "the identifying act of being that is the Word."[48] So far, so good. The relationship between the "divine subsistence" of the Word and the "human identity" of Jesus is not "competitive."[49] But this raises the question of whether, as Williams argues, "all the questions of Christology across the centuries begin with the deeply problematic and unused set of linguistic habits in the earliest Christian communities."[50] Though I think this is seriously questionable in terms of a reading of Christian theological history, my immediate concern is with how Christology (as Williams understands it) relates to the fear of God. Part of what is "overwhelming" about God, as we shall see in the next section, is that "the sheer radical otherness of God" is actually experienced to an extent by likenesses—such as we are.[51] When we know and experience ourselves to be such likenesses, we too tremble as did Paul and Silas' jailor, recognizing that our being is not our own, and that we are because another *is*. Being born anew is in part about an ever-intensifying awareness of our relatedness, nourished by Word and sacrament. In this respect, we can go some of the way with Williams, applauding his argument that, basically, the life of Jesus is what it is because of the Word. Also, we applaud his sense of the relevance of an account of God the Creator for "christological reflection."[52] Christology is downstream of the doctrine of God in terms of doctrinal architectonics. A robust account of the fear of God receives strengthening from Williams' account insofar as we do not relate to God "*in the same way*" as God relates to us. God is not and therefore does not relate to us as a composite reality, as if God were either animated or actualized by anyone or anything.[53] Instead, we tremble before one who does not relate to us as if he were a creature—that is, as one who has existence via participation in God. Unlike the Word, we are not "fully identical with the entirety of divine life as far as its qualities go."[54] But herein we receive further impetus to fear God, sensing the ever-greater dissimilarity between God and ourselves as likenesses. We fear God as believers because we receive in Christ forgiveness of sins, and thus a restoration of our nature.[55] We become new creations. Even then, however, we learn to exist no longer in relation to ourselves but as new creations. "Basic constraints" remain intact; our basic structure as creatures is unchanged.[56] What changes, however, is the way in which we experience ourselves as created. We experience ourselves as those who have nothing in relationship to themselves. We accept that all we are is of and for another. We repent. We do lovingly depend on the Father. But we love reverently, in fear. The more we imitate God, becoming the likenesses we are, the stiller we become before him, joining with "myriads of myriads," singing with full force to "the Lamb that was slaughtered" (Rev 5:12).

Williams' point about the human *esse* contributing nothing to the Word is relevant here. We contribute nothing to ourselves as far as our being is concerned. We are made. Therefore, we fear our Maker. Brief engagement with Sonderegger and Williams helps us to indwell this foundational point. Without the doctrine of participation doing extensive work, we diminish the possibilities available to us in terms of how the very structure of creatureliness encourages fear of God.

Jesus and Fear

We draw this chapter to a close by considering in a more speculative sense the Lord Jesus' fear of God. We do so because it so nicely ties the threads of this chapter together. Thomas argues, in *ST* 3.7.6, that what Christ "did fear was all that is overwhelming in God."

What is most overwhelming in God is God's thrice-holy goodness. What Thomas calls "the overwhelming good [is] to be found
in God." This is fear's foundation, the overwhelming goodness of
God. As we noted at the beginning of the chapter, fear has to do
with an awareness of being created, and creation as such is a participation via likeness in God's goodness. The created order shares, in
a participatory way understood analogously, in the absolute goodness of the one God, creator of heaven and earth. So far, so good.
But there is more, for Thomas introduces a new dimension to our
treatment of fear, one not found, explicitly anyhow, in the text of
Scripture itself. Thomas refers to fear in terms of a gift specific to
Christ's soul. Christ's "soul was moved, under the impulse of the
Holy Spirit, to a sense of reverence for God." Jesus Christ, while
blessed always with vision of the Father under the impulse of the
Spirit, "was also a pilgrim."[57] Jesus, like the individual Christian,
was, in his earthly ministry, a pilgrim, moved by the Spirit to revere
the Father. Pilgrims are pilgrims in relationship to what is above
them, and that is God. The individual Christian has, in terms of
their relationship to Jesus himself, a status that he or she shares
with them. We are just as Jesus was, a pilgrim, even though, unlike
us, Jesus always enjoyed the beatific vision as a pilgrim. That said,
Jesus "receives [from God] as man," and so all that Jesus receives
as man is gift, including the gift of the fear of God. Now, and not
surprisingly, there is a great deal of doctrinal delicacy in all this,
for Thomas links gifts with virtues. Gifts, specifically, "develop the
faculties of the soul in accordance with the prompting of the Holy
Spirit."[58] The gift of fear in Christ, prompted as it were by the Spirit,
is something that he receives as a pilgrim. And what he receives
awakens in him "a sense of reverence for God."

This is, I think, a different kind of fear than that said of the
ancestors in Paul's speech in Antioch of Pisidia in Acts 13:16–41.
The ancestors' fear is not connected, as is Christ's, to "the impulse
of the Spirit." This is because the ancestors' soul, as is the case with
every individual other than Christ, is not "united to the divinity."
The soul of Jesus is united to the divine Son of God by nature,
whereas our soul is, if we are believers, united to God by grace.

Jesus, accordingly, never ceases to revere God, for his soul is united to his divine person. We do not, in this life, revere God as Jesus does, for the God he reveres, his Father, he also sees, and all of that as a pilgrim. Jesus' human nature lacks nothing; he is not in need of grace, for all gifts are his, though he is nonetheless moved by the Spirit to revere the Father. This is (again) not true of us. Our fear is anchored in an often—at times—inchoate sense of our createdness and of our Creator, whereas Christ's reverence expresses his one person as subsisting in two natures. Things are different with us. Our fear of God must be perfected, and the way in which God perfects it is by the virtues that, as Thomas argues, "flow from grace."[59] Virtue, flowing from grace, makes conduct good.[60] We, unlike Christ, are to then become virtuous. Our fear, our reverence for God, grounded as it is in a sense of God pervading everything, must be perfected by grace. This happens as we imitate more and more the example of our Lord.[61]

How exactly is fear perfected? Fear is perfected among us by the virtue of mercy. Mercy, as discussed in chapter 1, is of God. That is where we began. And God communicates mercy to us, due to his great grace such that our conduct is made good and our defects removed. We no longer act for ourselves but in Christ, in order that he may be glorified and loved. As Ambrose notes, "Nothing commends the Christian soul so much as mercy."[62]

Mercy is indeed appropriate to our reverence of God. The merciful are blessed, says Jesus in Matthew 5:7, for it is they who recognize that the gifts of the Spirit that would perfect our humanity in relationship to Christ are desperately needed by us. We fall short, dramatically so. Therefore we must be merciful as God is merciful to us in Jesus Christ. The perfection our Lord commends leads us to great humility before God. Like Christ himself, we begin to appreciate how drastically preeminent God is, and therefore how much greater he is (John 14:32). Therefore, we, as those in need of mercy before the ultimate principle of being itself, must be merciful, too.[63]

And so, as we wrap up consideration of the fear of God in relationship to Christ and in relationship to the fear of God more broadly, we see the appropriateness of imitating Christ. He is our model, pattern, and guide in the fear of God. As Thomas notes, "As man Christ had a deeper sense of reverence for God than any other man." The pattern and form that fear of God takes is, ultimately, Jesus Christ. His fear is not "slavish fear, the kind that thinks mainly about punishment."[64] The perfect love of the man Jesus for the Father is rooted in and nourished by filial love. Filial love and its basis fear, as with mercy, "has God as its point of reference."[65] Filial fear, Thomas notes, "thus operates above the human mode and for this reason is a gift."[66] The fear of God, established upon the absolute preeminence of God, is in harmony with mercy. Mercy together with fear reminds us that God is ever greater, profoundly undomesticated, his mercy wider and more costly (to God) than hitherto imaginable. The gift of fear, as with the gifts of the Spirit in general, is a disposition from above, one that inclines us toward a deeper and deeper sense of reverence, following in the steps of our Lord Jesus himself.

To conclude, let us recall where Acts ends, namely with Paul under house arrest in Rome, his mission there being something of a failure, for, as with Peter's first speech, dullness of heart continues to pervade his people. And yet, that dullness occasions, for Paul, great confidence in God's salvation garnering a hearing among Gentiles. God is sovereign with respect to unbelief. God's absolute perfection accomplishes his promise to Abraham and his ancestors in the most unusual of ways, that is, by pronouncing judgment upon their infidelity, and using their infidelity—their greatest deficiency—as the means by which the proclamation of salvation reaches the Gentiles. This calls forth awe, best expressed with Paul's own words as found in Romans 11:25–36. We fear a God whose "judgments are unsearchable and ways inscrutable." It is not accidental that Paul's subtlest treatment of his own people's 'No' as the means to their salvation (via the engrafting of the Gentiles) evokes in Romans 9–11 the strongest possible sense of God's terrifyingly good grandeur: "For who has known the mind of the Lord? Or who has been his counsellor? Or who has given a gift to him, to receive a gift in return" (Rom 11:34–35)? The God and

Father of our Lord Jesus, he is the one to whom fear is directed in accordance with his image, Jesus himself, who exemplifies a life of reverent submission.

We end the treatment of fear, then, in the most remarkable place. We hear the Holy Spirit once again speaking. Just as Peter's first speech refers to the Spirit's speaking through David contextualizing as it were Judas' apostasy, we end with Paul speaking about the correctness of the Spirit's speaking through Isaiah, illuminating not just one Israelite's apostasy—that is, Judas'—but a whole people's apostasy. This is, in the end, the grounds for fearing God. God is sovereign over, indeed preeminent with respect to, apostasy, having no need of it but using it as the means by which the nations are blessed in accordance with the promise. The saving revelation of God "*masters* its environment."[67] The Spirit speaking through David and Isaiah provides the principle of intelligibility for apostasy. Apostasy before this God is not abolished in any immediate sense, for God permits it as the means by which God's salvation reaches the end of the earth, at least until Christ comes again to judge the living and the dead. Hard-heartedness is mastered. It is not perfected but shown to be utterly vain and futile in light of God's promise to manifest visibly and to all his kingdom of light and life.

6

Other Principal Points of Heavenly Teaching

I t is hoped that the reader will have by now been able to enter this scriptural book, "enveloped in mysteries" as it is.[1] The speech's subject matter is, as I have been indicating all along, God. Mercy, grace, hope, invocation, and fear are treated in relation to God. In this last major chapter, I discuss three doctrinal themes that warrant a more ordered discussion in a key that is at once experiential, ascetical, and contemplative. These themes are the raising of Jesus, the pouring out of the Spirit, and the church. The first theme draws on both Peter and Paul's speeches, the second Peter's speeches, and the third mostly Paul's, befitting as the letter does Paul's Gentile mission. I show not only how the contours of these great themes are gifts of God's love but also in what ways these themes might be inhabited as gifts of God's love, and only then described theoretically. Indeed, I theologize in relationship to these motifs as "an aspect of my life as a member of the Body of Christ."[2] Thus I place myself and the reader "under not only an academic but spiritual ascesis," showing how these themes as presented to us in Acts warrant not only systematic rigor but also ascetic discipline, nothing less.[3]

The forthcoming exploration of these themes will be somewhat speculative. I mean to comment on them in a way that is reflective of their divine orientation. One reason why the book of Acts is so strange to us is because of the ubiquity of God, God as one who speaks and acts throughout. But not only is Acts full of divine speaking and acting—of "a work that you will never believe"—it is also pregnant with divine silence of a sort (Acts 13:41). This silence is intelligible in relation to God's immense displeasure with his people's infidelity.[4] God is present in ways intervention-ist and, equally, in ways bespeaking silence, condoning thereby the judgment of a people who consider themselves "to be unwor-thy of eternal life" (13:46). Even in turning away, however, God is no less present, for in such a turning, a clear and devastating NO is uttered toward his people's apostasy. Apostasy becomes the instrument by which his promise is fulfilled.

The Resurrection

We begin with the resurrection. Peter's maiden speech reminds us that Matthias, chosen to replace Judas, "must become a witness with us to his resurrection" (Acts 1:22). What points does a theo-centric account of the resurrection emphasize, and what kind of ascesis does it encourage? These are my concerns in this section.

First, we remember that the resurrected one bears in his humanity unto all eternity Jewish and Gentile rejection of him. His glorified humanity includes our rejection of him. This signals something extraordinary about his divinity, indeed about what he is, divinity itself. Thomas writes, "The Godhead was united with Christ's flesh after death by personal union, but not by natural union." The man Jesus, raised from the dead, is personally united with the Godhead. The Son of God, God the Father's eternally beloved, has unto all eternity this form, the form of the risen man Jesus. Jesus' risen flesh is personally united to Godhead, the God-head of the Son. A supernaturally charged account of the resur-rection assumes just this, the personal union of Christ's flesh with Godhead, engendering what Thomas calls "a higher condition of nature." As always, Thomas is subtle, but his subtlety helps us appreciate what is so arresting about the proclamation of the one raised up. The resurrection does not denote an improvement on the part of Christ's person, some kind of "higher personal state." The risen Jesus is not more divine, more united with Godhead than before. To be sure, Jesus' resurrected body enjoys "a higher condition" as the first fruits and anticipation of the eschatological general resurrection. This is a very public reversal of entropic forces culminating in death.[5] The resurrection of Jesus is "the beginning and exemplar of all good things." This is why apostolic preaching witnesses to his resurrection and not so much his passion and death. Yes, the resurrection assumes his passion, but his passion and death that save "by removing evils" are not generative of apostolic proclamation in the way that Christ's resurrection is.[6] Why? The one raised enjoys "a higher condition of nature." The personal union of Godhead with flesh in the man Jesus does not destroy his bodily nature but uplifts it "as the beginning and exemplar of all good things."[7] Such a Thomistic perspective illuminates the precedence of the resurrection in apostolic preaching. Approaching the resurrection as the generative and structuring principle of all that is good here and now and in heaven is coextensive with a theocentric orientation. All good that comes to the world from God comes through his risen Son, who, together with God the Father and Spirit, is the greatest good.

As we contemplate the multiplicity of the references to the resurrection in Acts, what is extraordinary is that, unlike in John's Gospel, Jesus is never said to raise himself (John 2:13–25). Does this represent a subtle diminution of Jesus' divinity and of Godhead? Does this supply us with grounds for receiving his resurrection with a less than robust theocentric orientation? By no means! Thomas reminds us that there are two aspects of consideration when it comes to the resurrection: "first, in respect of His Godhead; secondly, in respect of His created nature." Acts emphasizes the second, "consider[ing] the body and soul of the dead Christ according to the power of created nature," whereas John emphasizes the first.[8] A naturalized account of the resurrection would privilege one respect—"His [Jesus'] created nature"—over and against His Godhead or, worse, ignore his Godhead altogether. It might also suggest that these emphases as represented by Acts and John compete with one another. Acts discourages such thinking, for God's power, divine power, raises the human Jesus, demonstrating as it were his divinity. Divine power has a precise Trinitarian reference. It is not logically inconsistent, then, to say that Jesus Christ was raised by God's power (as does Acts) and "by His own power" as is the case with John, though there is (again) more attention to this latter theme in John than in Acts.[9] Faith confesses that the Godhead is united to Christ's soul, which makes it "more powerful than the body in respect of its created nature."[10] This provides the grounds for saying that Jesus raises himself. Godhead is preeminent, then, whereas a naturalistic approach would leave us only with "created nature."[11] Thankfully, however, Jesus' resurrection shows us that God's power is common to the Father and Son. Therefore, when we preach that God raised him, following Acts' lead, we preach the priority of God, who is the key to understanding the Son's Godhead and his created nature.

If we were to approach these mysteries without God, we might think that Jesus' resurrection led to some kind of development in his person. We might adjudge that the resurrection adds something essential to him, what Thomas refers to as an "increase in the glory of his body or of his soul." Neither Christ's resurrection nor his ascension, however, adds something to him. Yes, the man Jesus ascends; he is lifted up. He is no longer physically present, but he is nonetheless spiritually present in the hearts of the baptized, in the preached word and the sacred Supper. The resurrection *confirms* Christ's divinity, and the ascension shows us how Christ, though bodily absent, is present according to his divinity and in the Holy Spirit. The resurrected Jesus is present not according to his body but according to his divinity. A theocentrically charged account of the resurrection recognizes that the lack of Christ's bodily presence (aside from the Eucharist) is among us not a sign of his being bound by alien laws. Instead, it denotes that the human nature he assumes is mobile in relation to him. The Son assumes a human nature without destroying it, fitting it out for heaven as an act of his supreme power. Faith sees in this a great hope: that we might attain heaven too for Jesus has gone there and poured out his Spirit in such a way that we might also ascend there.

This is important to meditate upon as it helps us understand why Acts is rather quiet about the ongoing activity of the resurrected Jesus. This is explained, in part, with reference to a helpful comment that Augustine makes: *"For although Christ's bodily presence left us, we have spiritually present Father, Son, and Holy Spirit."*[12] The Trinity is present in Acts, spiritually, following Jesus' being lifted up. The main person present and at work in the narrative is the Father, with the Spirit being a close second. It is God the Father's presence and agency that are most prominent in the narrative. The resurrected and ascended Jesus is also present, albeit in a twofold form. First, Jesus is present in the preaching of Peter and Paul; Jesus is present via their declaration that God raised him. In other words, Jesus is present as the one raised and lifted up. Second, Jesus is present in the form of his name, healing and exorcising. It is in Jesus' name that Peter exorcises the demon from the fortune-telling "slave-girl" in Acts 16:16–40, and it is in Jesus' name that the lame man in 3:1–10 walks. This risen and ascended Jesus—God's one and only Son—is present, first and spiritually, at the center of the apostles' preaching, whether to Jews or Gentiles, and, secondly, through healing and exorcising undertaken in his name.

The man Jesus is raised as God, publicly vindicated by God, manifest to all as God's eternally begotten Son. He is raised by the Father as God, shown to be the Father's only beloved, and thereby raises our nature, the "earthly nature in the unity of his person."[13] Therefore, when we consider the resurrection, we also see in the resurrected Jesus the very resurrection of our earthly nature. We see ourselves in him and where we will be. But the agent of Christ's being raised and of our being raised in him is God. Though (again) another New Testament writer—John—points in John 2:13–25 to Christ as the one who raises himself, Acts uniformly stresses that God raises the man Jesus, and bodily, and that he is lifted up "to a given space" where God pours out through him the Spirit.[14] Resurrection in Acts, then, is profoundly Trinitarian. The Father raises, and the one raised is he through whom God the Spirit, "the gift of God," is poured out (Acts 2:38).

What Acts teaches, then, is a basic theocentric truth. The body of the man Jesus is raised, and raised because "it is personally united to God."[15] The hypostatic union is the principle of the resurrection. Even more, the Father's raising has its ground in the eternal generation of the Son. The Father raises the Son because the Son is eternally begotten of him. The resurrection confirms to both Jews and Gentiles a common horizon, namely, that God will judge the world through this man who, in being raised, is attested to be God. This man is no mere man, a mortal, but "God in heaven."[16] What follows from this glorious truth is reverence. Herein we see the ascetical dimension of teaching on the resurrection. Jesus' resurrection, in demonstrating his divinity, increases reverence; for Christ, in being raised, leads us to a place that does not merely exceed our nature but is "foreign" to it.[17] We are not, naturally, capable of heaven, let alone "citizens" of it (Phil 3:20). But even then, we who remain here revere him. Though Acts does not discuss this, Jesus is also, by virtue of his assuming and exalting human nature into heaven, interceding for us. In Thomas' exceptional words, "The presence of his human nature in heaven is itself an intercession for us."[18] His humanity, risen and ascended, is intercessory humanity. We revere him, who intercedes for us.

To expand (briefly) the first of our principal points of heavenly teaching, we consider Christ's descent to Paul in Acts 9:1–9. There, we see, though perhaps with even greater clarity than in 2:23–24, that the man crucified is raised in glory because he is united "to the divinity."[19] Jesus cannot be held in death's power because he is united to divinity as one who is, personally, the Son of God himself. The resurrection conveys a principal teaching: Christ is divine; therefore, "God raised him up" (2:24). And the reason God did so is because this Jesus is his eternally beloved Son, one with himself (and the Spirit) from and to eternity. At the heart of the gospel's spread throughout the latter first-century Greco-Roman world is the truth that blinds Saul. Jesus Christ appears as "light from heaven" for he *is* "light from heaven" (9:3). What are you, Jesus? I am light from heaven. Who are you, Jesus? "I am." Saul had hitherto assumed that Jesus was dead. What Saul discovers, on the road, is that Jesus Christ was raised, receiving "by the resurrection that quality of glory called clarity."[20] Jesus uses Saul's unbelief to manifest his risen glory, appearing to Saul in shocking clarity. The only form of life commensurate with this glorious revelation is reverent witness. This will entail, in Saul's case, suffering.[21]

Does witness, the first fruit of faith, necessarily entail suffering? While it certainly does for Saul more so than most, Saul's commission is common to all believers. Disciples are to bring forward Jesus' name, though the form that Paul's bringing forth takes is particularly transparent to suffering. But even then, the "I am" who appears to Saul sends Saul the Holy Spirit, who fills him and remedies his blindness, providing comfort on the journey.

There is a distinctive spirituality appropriate to Acts, anchored in Peter's declaration of Jesus' resurrection and ascension, and of God pouring out the Spirit through Jesus. It takes its cues from Jesus. Jesus is one with the Spirit. He is "the Spirit-baptizer" because he receives the Spirit from all eternity as the Father's only begotten and beloved Son.[22] Accordingly, Jesus provides the gift of the Spirit because "*spirituality* is a property of the glorious body."[23] Spirituality is not accidental to Jesus' glorified body but proper to it. Accordingly, in living spiritually, we live according to his form, his glorious body. Spirituality is something we receive, and the one from whom we receive it is our model, leader, and guide. He infuses us with his Spirit in baptism, and through the sacred Supper he gives us grace to be subject in all things to the will of the Spirit. If Thomas is right, as I think he is, a spirituality appropriate to Jesus' being raised will take its cues from the ascension. It is the ascended Christ whose glorious body is the subject and agent (in the Spirit) of true spirituality.

The Pouring Out of the Spirit

Jesus Christ—risen, ascended, and glorified—pours out the Spirit. What does this reveal about God's inner life? The Spirit whom God gives through Jesus God receives from no one, whereas Jesus receives the Spirit eternally and in time from God. Believers (either Jewish or Gentile), in turn, receive the Spirit from God in a manner simultaneous with their believing in the Lord Jesus. In believing in Jesus and in being baptized, the believers receive the Spirit. As we read Acts, we see that the Gentiles do not believe in the Spirit and thereby receive Jesus. Faith has a clear Christo-centric orientation. Why is the Spirit given, then? That the risen, ascended, and glorified Jesus might reign in us, "God's eschatolog-ical people."[24] The shape of the Spirit's work as gift is Christ's reign, his kingdom. The gift given imparts to us the capacity to live in accord with the reign of Jesus. What is the principal point of such teaching? The Spirit is given in order that Christ might indwell, transform, and transfigure us.

Is there an ascetical dimension to God's giving this great gift? If so, what kind of people ought we to be? We ought, I think, to be an evangelizing people, confident in the self-authenticating power of the good news. Evangelism is part and parcel of what it means to be God's eschatological people, a people who are recipients of the great gift, the Holy Spirit. Evangelizing people are certain sorts and kinds of people. An evangelizing people are a people who, driven by the Spirit, cease hindering God. We hinder God when we eat, for example, with only a select or certain few, dis-regarding what makes for harmonious table fellowship between Jews and Gentiles. We hinder God when we think that we are at least partly responsible for effecting the repentance that leads to life. That is God's business, but we too have business, and that is the business of believing and of bearing witness—which is what it means to evangelize in relation to the Lord Jesus. Witness to Jesus assumes supernatural wonder, indeed the great surprise Luke describes in Acts 10:45. This is the astonishment that the Spirit happily falls on those Gentiles who hear "the word" (10:44). This astonishment has evangelical power, accompanied as it may be by tongues, signs, and marvels. Intrinsic to the ascetics of evangelism is a willingness to hear and, perhaps, to stop, as Peter says, hindering God. This is a hearing that births silence, a silence that, in due course, erupts in praise to God. If academic theology is to "be of use to the Church in its tremendous pastoral and evangelistic task," it must encourage such eruptions of praise.[25]

The church's evangelistic task assumes speaking the word. The church has a word to proclaim. The word proclaimed is Jesus Christ risen from the dead. People cannot attain, as did Stephen, a vision of Christ unless they hear the message regarding him. The message has evangelical power because, as we see with Peter's speaking to the Gentiles in Acts 10 and his report on that to the church at Jerusalem in Acts 11, when the apostolic word is spoken, the Spirit falls. When Jesus is preached, Jesus pours out the promise he receives from the Father. This is (again) why the good news has enormous power. Thus, the church approaches its evangelistic task with confidence knowing that its message is spiritual, coextensive with the gift of the Holy Spirit, who freely falls and blows where he will.

Hearing involves faith. Hearing pertains to faith, notes Thomas, and hearing involves us agreeing with God that it is he, and not we ourselves, who is the Lord. The Lord may allow us to be "unbearably crushed" (2 Cor 1:8) in order that we might learn dependence, and an ever-greater appreciation of the consolation awaiting us, that of "unending presence."[26] The dependence we learn is also a sort of scriptural dependence. Scripture is, after all, "the foundation of faith."[27] Scriptural faith instructs us via the Mosaic and prophetic testimony about Christ "that everyone who believes in him receives forgiveness of sins through his name" (Acts 10:42). Moses and the prophets speak Christ, and Christ pours out the Spirit, that we might hear him speak through Moses and the prophets and respond in faith and in turn encourage others to listen in faith.

The invisible Spirit whom Jesus pours out enables us to believe in the Lord Jesus, whom we cannot see but who wills to be heard. We believe in him, who is ascended and glorified, and we become by believing increasingly transparent to his work in all its evangelical and spiritual power. We believe without seeing, but not without hearing, the word through whom the Spirit falls. The Spirit alone enables experience of that same word. We may be alive to the word only in the Spirit.

The resurrected and ascended state of Jesus is one of glory. This is the glory that blinds Paul and astonishes those who hear the word. The apostle Peter (and Paul as well) is too careful a theologian to assume that we will immediately appreciate that the Lord Jesus in his exalted glory is, in fact, God. That Jesus pours out "the same gift" is because he is God, personally united, as we noted earlier, to God the Son. Jesus' exaltation in God is, however, not a truth that we simply acknowledge. It is, instead, one to which we are led. Thus, Peter's speeches to the Israelites have as their basis God's covenantal history with his people. For example, in preaching to the Israelites in Solomon's Portico in Acts 3:12–26, Peter begins (of course) with Jesus, "whom God raised from the dead," but moves in the second half of the speech to the prophets and indeed to the promise made to Abraham, the treatment of which is bookended by the trope "when God raised up his servant" (3:15, 26). This suggests not only simply a rhetorical strategy but also how we must be led gently toward recognition of Christ's state of glory.[28] Christ ascends to the Father in the Spirit and, as exalted, receives the Spirit from the Father. For us to see with the eyes of faith what this implies regarding Christ's divinity and indeed the Spirit's, we must be led spiritually "*in an intimate, progressive way*," notes Augustine, to recognize the "*equality between Father and Son*."[29] We see progressively the trinitarian logic of Peter's speeches insofar as we are led to inhabit them, spiritually. The Spirit poured out leads us to Jesus in such a way that we might believe in him, as did the Gentiles in Acts 10 and 11. The Spirit falls on us so as to lift up our hearts and minds to where Christ is. It is the Lord Jesus who leads by the Spirit, often in quite extraordinary ways. The Lord sends angels and pours out his Spirit that we might speak his word. But even then, we must be sober with respect to the quality of our faith and hearing, for we may, even in the midst of prayer, fail to recognize God's work among us. We may think that some of those among us, like Rhoda of old, are out of their mind as they disclose news that is too great for us to apprehend (cf. Acts 12:6–19). Only when we believe and proclaim in the Spirit do we stand a chance of being intimately and progressively led to the amazement that the Lord's work among us evokes. Instead of ignoring the Rhodas among us, we welcome the news they bring with open hearts and minds, however bewildering it may be.

Perhaps the most fitting place in the narrative of Acts in which to consider the resurrection and the pouring out of the Spirit that accompanies Christ's ascension is Stephen's stoning. Therein the themes of resurrection and the pouring out of the Spirit as pursued in an ascetic key receive great stimulus. Stephen is, of all the characters we encounter in the narrative of Acts, the one who most clearly conforms himself to, as Thomas comments, "the model of Christ's passion and death in our own mortal lives." Christ's passion and death absorb Stephen's death, providing a portrait of sorts by which we appreciate the shape of Stephen's death. Stephen's martyrdom also helps us to integrate our themes of resurrection and the Spirit's pouring out. Stephen dies as Jesus dies. Stephen's death observes the order that exists with respect to, first, Christ's death and, second, Christ's resurrection. First, we must be conformed to Christ's death and, second, strive for what Thomas calls "a participation in the likeness of Christ's resurrection."[30] This needs to be carefully unfolded. Conformation to Christ's death precedes participation in his resurrection. We must conform ourselves to a model, that model being Jesus, something that Stephen does in the costliest of fashions. The fruit of that conformation is participation, but participation in what?

A likeness—but again, why not simply resurrection instead of "the likeness of his resurrection?" The keyword is mortal. Christ is raised to immortal life, whereas when we die, assuming that we have conformed ourselves to the model of Christ's death in our earthly lives, our soul is joined to Christ. Our soul, though outwardly our bodies are wasting away, participates in a likeness of Christ's resurrection insofar as it is being renewed day by day. Christ's resurrection may only be said to be a model of our own resurrection if we, following Stephen's example, "become conformed to the image of his own sonship."[31] Our bodily resurrection to life when Christ comes again, as the one whom God has appointed to judge the living and the dead, is conditional upon our conformation to his death. Though we hope that there will be "universal restoration," that hope is always expressed as a prayer (Acts 3:21). Good people must pray for it without assuming its givenness. It remains a hope. When we conform ourselves to Christ's death, his resurrection becomes the exemplary cause of our own. This does not detract from the devastating reality of bodily death. Our participation in Christ's resurrection is, after all, that of a likeness. And that likeness is twofold. Stephen dies, and his soul is resurrected. His bodily resurrection awaits Christ's coming again in glory. Accordingly, Christ's resurrection is unlike ours, for Christ dies and is raised, bodily, from the dead. His body is united to his soul on the third day. This is not true of Stephen and certainly not of us. Christ's resurrection has an efficacy and range all its own. Because Jesus is divine, he raises our souls and, at the end of time, bodies "through the divine power which he has from his personal union with the divinity."[32] Stephen, of course, is not personally united with divinity. And yet, Stephen's body and soul belong in death to God and should experience a reunion of sorts when Christ comes again.

Herein lies the basis for the Son's divinization and our own. We are raised according to God's substance. Our soul's resurrection, notes Thomas, "belongs to God's substance," meaning that what is proper to God is that in which our resurrected soul participates as well as our bodies, though not until the end of time. Note the direction, though: we participate, yes, but we are not thereby absorbed as it were into God. Also, God does not participate in us. God's substance is that in which we participate but never the reverse—the direction is always from God to us. As Thomas writes, "The soul participates in God's divine good and becomes just and good."[33] The participation the resurrected soul enjoys is utterly transformative. Stephen remains Stephen, his soul and body perfected by their participation in divine goodness, becoming "just and good," though with Stephen there is rather less becoming to take place than with most of us, I suspect. This also means that there is a sort of spiritual purification that takes place in the interim state between death (and thus the soul's resurrection with Christ) and the soul's being joined to the body in the end-time resurrection. This suggests that "the efficacy of Christ's resurrection extends" to the soul first—Jesus receives Stephen's "spirit" upon death (Acts 7:59). When Jesus comes again, Stephen's soul will then be blessed with a resurrection body.

What does this infer regarding the relationship of the resurrection to the pouring out of the Spirit? As we look to Paul's speeches, what surprises us is the lack of any reference to the Spirit in Paul's first speech to "the Israelites" in the synagogue at Antioch in Acts 13:16–41. While the refrain "But God raised him from the dead" anchors Paul's narration of his own people's apostate history, there is no mention of the Spirit. There is, though, mention of the turn to the Gentiles in light of the Jews' rejection, though of course that rejection does not cover all Jews—"many Jews and devout converts to Judaism followed Paul and Barnabas" (13:43). Even as Paul goes to the Gentiles, he does not forsake the synagogue, as was the case in Thessalonica. But again what is interesting is that it is the Messiah's death and resurrection, as explained and proved by the Scriptures, that animates Paul. Even in Paul's first sermon to the Gentiles in Acts 17:16–31, which unfolds "the good news about Jesus and the resurrection," appealing as it does to the witness of the created order and of our common descent from

Adam, Paul emphasizes the day of eschatological judgment by the resurrected man appointed to judge. But again, no mention is made of the Holy Spirit, the pouring out of which is, as we saw, a prevalent theme (or at least a more prevalent theme) in Peter's speeches (17:18). However, in Acts 17:16–31, God raises so as to judge.[34] Indeed, God does not raise Jesus so as to pour out the Spirit—though this is not wrong to suggest. Instead, God raises up Jesus, and the Spirit witnesses to Jesus' exaltation by God as judge of all, living and dead. What does this imply for scriptural consideration of the Spirit's person and work in relation to the resurrected Jesus? There must be a certain proportion maintained in terms of our consideration of the one triune God and his work. God the Father has a certain priority as the fount of divinity in the order of origin as expressed in the missions of the Son and Spirit. Jesus and the Spirit are God, and yet they are ordered to the Father as (again) the fount of divinity. A Christology and a pneumatology that is neither overinflated nor underinflated must respect this. The priority, the weight as it were, is upon the Father, though this does not mean for a moment that the Son and Spirit are less divine, possessing less Godhead, if I may put it that way. That said, the Father in the narrative is the subject of the action, whereas the Son is raised and the Spirit is poured out from God through the one raised. The Spirit receives from the Father, for the Spirit is from the Father, and never the reverse. The resurrection and the Spirit poured out point to God's preeminence, just as does the created order and the eschatological judgment of all. As we consider the speeches in all their grandeur, we see that there is an unrelenting, spiritually demanding even, concentration on God (the Father).

The Church of God

How does this relate to thinking about the church? What does Acts teach about the church, and what kind of spiritual ascesis is demanded by that teaching? "The church of God" is obtained by the blood of God's Son (Acts 20:21).[35] God gets a hold of the

church via his Son (20:21).[36] The church is "of God," just as is
the case with the resurrection of Christ and the gift of the Spirit
poured out. What is the logic behind this? Why then does Paul
not say the church "of Christ?" Similarly, we might ask why Christ
is described by Paul as the "head" of the church and not God?
Well, as with the Spirit, the church is of God but through Christ.
Christ is the body's head, and Christ as the head confers upon the
church "what has been conferred upon him."[37] We receive from
Christ the gift of eternal life and thus the forgiveness of sin, the
fruit of which is participation in the divine nature. Again, this is
the point made a moment ago about divinization. Christ confers
life not only because he was raised to immortal life but because he
is life itself. Life is his, the same life proper to the Father and Spirit
by dint of their one essence. Christ, as the head of the body, sets
"free from all those sins from which you could not be freed by the
law of Moses" (13:39). As crucial as it is to be free from sin, such
liberation is not an end in itself, for Christ frees us from sin so as
to renew us in relation to God. Because the man Jesus is himself
united to the Word, he confers upon us what is his, essentially
speaking. But again, he is the head, but God is the goal. And it is
in this sense that the church is "of God." We follow Jesus and, in
so doing, are led by him to divine things. We will never be personally united with the Word as Jesus is—by nature—but we—by
grace—receive what he receives from the Father, including the
grace of sonship. Through Christ we receive the gift of participation in God. As Thomas says, "God alone makes souls happy
through participation in him."[38] Christ's headship with respect to
the church, then, concerns end-time bodily resurrection. Yes, he
in his incarnation assumes human nature so as to unite it to God.
We again are not personally united to God as he is, but we (the
believing community) share in what he receives from the Father,
including the Spirit. The Son receives everything from the Father
(except the Father's being Father), and what he receives, we too
receive. But we receive as creatures, whereas Christ receives both
as God and as man.

What Jesus Christ the incarnate Lord and the church have in common is that they are both "of God" though God is not of them; Christ's humanity and the church derive from God, whereas God is not ordered in an ontological sense to them. Christ as man (a man who indeed is God) dies for us, obtaining the church with his own blood. He is its head, and to persecute the body is to persecute the head. In beating those who believe, Saul, as we said, persecutes Jesus himself. As Mascall notes, "Jesus cannot be detached from the Church which is his Bride and his Body, the People of God, the New Israel."[39] The one church of God of which Christ is the head has a twofold character in Acts, especially in Paul's speeches, that is illuminated by Chalcedonian logic. Paul locks "up many of the saints in prison," and yet it is Jesus he persecutes (Acts 26:10). Paul, however, neither identifies nor separates the saints and Jesus. The church is of God through Christ its head. Christ is the head of those who "receive forgiveness of sins and a place among those who are sanctified by faith in me" (26:18). Jesus Christ is this as the one who leads to God so that we may share in what God is, glorious goodness itself.

Another parallel involves Paul's language of "this salvation of God" and that of "the kingdom of God" (Acts 28:28). Jesus is the Savior and he is King—but his saving and ruling are of God. God is the principle of intelligibility for both salvation and the kingdom: both are of him. Jesus enacts salvation and is salvation; he too enacts the kingdom and is the kingdom. Jesus Christ is the head of God's church, but Jesus is not the head of God. All created things are *from* God, just as God the Father is also the fount of deity for Son and Spirit.

What kind of spiritual ascesis is warranted by the deep truth of the church being of God? We answer by saying that what is of God is that which is through Jesus. Paul convinces (or tries to convince) "the local leaders of the Jews" about Jesus "from the law of Moses and from the prophets" (Acts 28:17). Some of course agree, while an equal number disagree. Paul himself is not convinced until, as with Peter in John's Gospel, Jesus himself appears to him, addressing him personally. Indeed, Paul suffers Jesus' light, being blinded by it. Until Paul suffers the blindness-inducing presence of Christ, he does not realize that Moses and the prophets speak in relation to Jesus. Paul does not hear Jesus speak through them, and so he does not really appreciate that they are of God until he listens to Jesus. Paul has to learn to suffer afresh Jesus' testimony, to hear him speak where he did not think he could be heard, Moses and the prophets. Similarly, Paul must suffer the church of God. Paul has to suffer his own people's ignorance of their Messiah. Paul has to suffer the extraordinary truth that the church of God is through Jesus, indeed through Moses and the prophets as they witness to Jesus himself. Paul has to learn in the Spirit how to read Scripture afresh.

The church of God is through Jesus. Jesus is "the Way" to the Father according to John (14:6). "The Way" is also said of the church of God. Those against whom Paul breathes "threats and murder" belong to "the Way" (Acts 9:2). The church of God—the *way*—belongs to Jesus Christ—the *Way*. The way of Jesus is crucifixion and death. The whole way of "the Way" resembles the death that marks Peter's and Paul's ministries. Peter dies a kind of death he does not want to die (cf. John 21:15–19). Paul, too, ends his ministry in Rome in chains. There is a kind of narrowing in the narrative of Acts that helps us appreciate the character of the church of God described as "the Way." Acts ends with an apostle in chains, under house arrest, "for the sake of the hope of Israel" (Acts 28:20). The narrowing has to do with infidelity and apostasy. Acts' narrative is anything but triumphalist. We end with a declaration of corporate apostasy via Isaiah just as Peter began his first speech by contextualizing Judas' apostasy via the Holy Spirit's words spoken through David (28:26–27). Apostasy, the death of corporate commitment to listening, is where Acts ends. To belong to the Way in both its ecclesiological and christological sense is to own this dark reality. Israel's heart "has grown dull" (28:27). The Way is, however, not entirely composed of dull hearts. And yet, those belonging to the Way, as is evidenced perhaps most strongly in 1 Corinthians 5:1, are well marked by death. Yes, the Gentiles will listen, but their listening is hardly more disciplined than Israel's. Those belonging to the Way (in both senses), whether Jews or Gentiles, must die to the illusion that the sins of the ancestors are not sins from which they are, in principle, exempt. Truly belonging to the Way means dying to the fantasy that apostasy lives only then and there, in the ancestors' history.

A theocentric account of the church—"the church of God"—clarifies thinking regarding opposition to God. Because God is alive—so eternally alive and self-existent, "in need of nothing"—God raises Jesus. As a result, apostasy as the Way's mysterious nemesis lives. Acts takes the Satan, death, and apostasy as seriously as it does because of God, "the salvation of God" (Acts 28:28). Because the way (the believing community) belongs to *the* Way (Jesus Christ), its life is marked bearing the cross. And it is within the church of God that we learn how to die. This is the asceticism of the Way. Even the believing community's acknowledgment of its potential to turn away from God in ways great and small is key to its being of the Way. Those belonging to the way (the believing community), because they have given everything to the Way, let him take everything, including the community's own sense that it will be faithful. If the Old Testament is to live for us, we must see ourselves as being read by it. Indeed, and even stronger, we stand in it, as those who do what the ancestors did. The way (the believing community) preaches the Way (Jesus Christ) alert to the harsh reality of apostasy, of being on the receiving end of the Holy Spirit's words as recorded in Isaiah 28:26–28.

The Baptism of God

We might ask how God on a very practical level keeps us in the Way in such a way that we—the believing community—remain "of him."[40] I think the sacraments are key, most especially baptism. I say baptism because it is what believers (and the children of believers) undergo upon confessing Jesus; also, because it shapes the cruciform character of life in the church of God. Baptism washes sins away: "Get up, be baptized, and have your sins washed away, calling on his [Jesus'] name" (Acts 22:16). Baptism as the ritual event of cleansing in Jesus' name reminds us that belonging to the way involves ongoing baptism into the Way (Jesus Christ). When persons are baptized in the name of Jesus, they become believers in God and blessed with the regenerating Spirit of God. Moreover, the way that is Jesus Christ involves sight, the sight that is restored to us when we believe, receive the Spirit, and are baptized. Sight accompanies purity of heart. That the Holy Spirit enables not just hearing but sight attests this (e.g., Acts 2:33). We see—though I do not know how—the Spirit in Jesus. The Spirit's sight is of the Father whom we see in Jesus, Jesus being the one through whom the Spirit is poured out. Baptism cleanses our sight so that those of the way see the Way. Sight in the Spirit means seeing Jesus, and how do we see Jesus but through worshiping him, the foundation and shape of which is baptism.

Mascall provides us with a helpful insight regarding baptism's character that maps nicely onto baptism as practiced in Acts. Jesus, *the* Way into whom those belonging to the way are baptized, is present to the baptized. Jesus lives because God raised him, and therefore baptism into his name is baptism in his life and presence. The ascended Jesus Christ lives bodily, in a glorified body. His earthly body (the church) participates in his glorified body, and he is present to his earthly body in the Spirit. His earthly body is indeed perfected by his heavenly body through the (Eucharistic) renewal of the relation in which the church is set through baptism. Baptism in the name of Jesus denotes a new relation to Jesus—a believing one—and thus the way of initiation into his body, that to which the baptized now belongs. Accordingly, baptism is not about receiving a quantity of grace but again of being set "in a new relation to the church which is Christ's body."[41] Christ's body, the church, the "church of God," is, in Mascall's winsome words, "a permanent supernatural entity" precisely because of its being "a sacramental organism."[42] It is God almighty who through Jesus, in the power of the Spirit, sets persons like the Ethiopian eunuch in a new relation to Christ and his body, the church. And yet, God does this supernatural thing through natural means, that is, Philip as he expounds Isaiah's words in Acts 8:26–40; God does not compete with and exclude Philip; grace perfects our witness.

The church, as "a permanent enduring supernatural entity," thus depends on God for its beginning, that is, its baptism, and on God for its sustenance, that is, the Eucharist, which, as Mascall notes, "exists for the building and maintenance of the Body of Christ."[43] The Eucharist and therewith baptism are related to Christ as the one who cleanses us and sustains us through the visible signs of bread and wine. Jesus Christ does so in order that we might remain related to him and his body (those on the way) and thus be the people *of* God. Being set in relation to Christ in the waters of baptism and being renewed in that relation via the sacred Supper means that the church "is essentially outward looking and directed to others."[44] Just so, the fecundity of the church's baptism and its participation in the Supper means proclaiming Jesus' death until he comes again. Hence the evangelistic dimension discussed earlier and the kind of people such a call requires us to become. The church is directed to others as those for whom Christ has died and rose again. The church's motivation is love, God's love, and it is that which converts the intellectual, moral, and affective lives of the most hardened of sinners. Accordingly, the life of the baptized (whether in an individual or congregational sense) attests, witnesses, and manifests God, who in the Lord Jesus sets them in a new and friendship-inspiring relation to himself.

We grasp via baptism into Jesus' name something of the radical difference between his name and our own names. The name of Jesus is the name of God's one and only eternally existent and beloved Son. Jesus is not baptized by us, but we are by him, in his Spirit, and so recognize afresh our radical dependence on him. This does not mean the abolition of friendship with him and his Father, who is also our Father. What it does mean, however, is a fresh recognition of the compatibility of Creator and creature. We (creatures) are made for our Creator (who is unmade). Our created nature as humans is not abhorrent to him, thankfully, but is that through which Christ unites us to his person. The creature is compatible with the Creator in and through Christ, who, in cleansing us, uses the water of baptism to set us in a new relation to himself within the context of the family of God. Thus the church of God, the body of Christ, knows of no independence, no detachment as it were from Christ, who, through the renewal of our baptism into the sacred Supper, renders us more and more compatible with himself.

If such is the case, then, Jesus Christ attests and declares himself through the church's ministry of Word and sacrament, effective as it is in his Spirit. Christ enables the Church (like Scripture) to mediate his presence and truth. The church of God's relationship to Jesus Christ, whose body the church is, is not parallel with the relation of the divine Son to the human nature he assumes. We rightly speak of the theandric character of Jesus, that the man Jesus, his humanity, is "the medium and instrument" of the divine Son.[45] But the church, the body of Christ, the way as it were, is not a medium but again a witness, the way to *the* Way. The hypostatic union describes, nicely, the one eternal Word's union in his person of complete divinity and humanity. That said, the hypostatic union is not at all appropriate for describing Jesus' relation to his earthly body, the church. Though Jesus cannot be detached from his body, the church, Jesus is never said to receive from it insofar as his divinity is concerned. There is a strict asymmetry here between Christ and the church. Believers minister to Christ bodily through ministry to "the least of these," thereby "sharing" in Christ's sufferings (Matt 25:45; Phil 3:10). Just so, the "metaphysical subject" and "principal agent" in the human actions of Jesus is the person of the Word.[46] The church does not compete with him, but it does love him and conform to the relation into which baptism has placed it by loving the least. There is, I think, a need to always honor the truth that the church, as Christ's body, has Christ and its baptism into him as its principle and ongoing presupposition.

Thus when we consider the "church of God" in a register derivative of Acts and in an ascetic key, we appreciate the centrality of baptism as well as Eucharist as that into which we are baptized. The church preaches Jesus and baptizes in his name because there is nothing more proper to it. Jesus bends us toward himself, as our foundation, in his Spirit, through the waters of baptism, the hearing of the preached word, and our being sealed in its promises through the sacred Supper. Because the one into whose name we are baptized is God the Son, we are directed toward God through him, *the* Way. The "proper form" of Christ risen and ascended and glorified is the church, his body, the way, and it is he who through his Spirit is "the principle of its characteristic activity."[47] The body of Christ, the church of God, exists through its form, Jesus Christ himself, causing it to exist via its sharing in his sufferings and death.

Such sharing, remarkably, is anything but a burden. We come to delight in him to the extent that we die in him, and herein again the church receives its evangelical and catechetical zeal. What we delight in, "we wish *to share*," observes Thomas following Aristotle's lead.[48] And the reason why Paul welcomes as liberally as he does while under house arrest is because of the joy he receives from God's kingdom and "teaching about the Lord Jesus" (Acts 28:31). They are more precious to him than gold, and so he does not fume because of his arrest in Jerusalem and his being "handed over to the Romans" (28:17).

What Peter, Paul, and the apostles as a whole appreciate is, above all else, God, especially God's love. They desire others to receive that love in baptismal form, whether they be Jews or Gentiles. They know that God delights in making "known His love towards us."[49] This is the function, in part, of the sacraments. They are external signs by which God manifests his love for us and binds us in turn to the one who is love incarnate, Jesus Christ. Though Acts does not teach us everything about the sacraments—we have, obviously, little to work with in the case of the sacred Supper—we have nonetheless a reasonable amount of material regarding baptism. Baptism establishes for the new believer and convert the need for self-denial, the mortification of the flesh, and disciplined preoccupation with the life of the world to come. But even so, I think Calvin is right to say that "the grace of God is not tied to the sacraments."[50] And yet, the sacraments are where new life receives its form (baptism) and ongoing renewal (the Supper) in the proclaimed promises of God. Grace is not imprisoned in the sacrament of baptism but is nonetheless operative there. This has simply to do with Christ, who "is appointed to be the One prominent in baptism."[51] It is Christ's life, death, and resurrection into which we are baptized, and in being baptized into him we are baptized with his Spirit. Christ is the center of baptism: hence the apostles baptize in his name.

Not so with us, however, who baptize in the name of the Trinity, following the dominical command in Matthew 28:19. Jesus' commandment is an expansion, a rendering explicit of what was implicit in apostolic practice in Acts. Calvin comments, accordingly, that "invocation of the name of Christ includes in itself the Father and the Spirit." The same logic applies to baptism. Baptism in Jesus' name includes the Father and the Spirit, though again Christ is most prominent. The waters of baptism cleanse as they do not by virtue of their own power but because of "the power of Christ alone."[52] The "outward sign"—water—has power because of Christ. The efficacy of the sign is due to Christ. Is it then right to say that baptism as practiced by the apostles in Acts is the foundation of piety? Not quite. I think that faith in God takes precedence. Faith in God's salvation and God's kingdom has priority. We do not receive baptism and then faith, but faith and then baptism. The promises contained in baptism are rightly received in faith. Baptism gives faith its form, but baptism's foundation is again faith. Calvin is right to say that faith "is the one and only foundation of piety."[53] And it is correct to say as does Calvin that "by faith . . . we come to possess all the blessings which are offered through the Gospel."[54] At the same time, I think that what Calvin says is slightly inadequate. It is better to aver that faith possesses gospel blessings through baptism and is renewed in them through the sacred Supper. Again, what Calvin states is not false; rather, it is somewhat incomplete. Faith is the appointed instrument through which we possess all gospel blessings; the form in which we, as it were, possess them is baptism, and our renewal in them is the Supper.

Such an account of the church avoids attributing to the church any realizing function. On the one hand, as Williams makes clear with respect to the incarnation, the incarnation renders "human nature capable of a new level of 'hypostatic' agency in respect of the whole entire created order."[55] This reorients "the structure of human nature . . . towards realizing in the finite world the character or quality of the *infinite* reality which is the Word's loving dependence on the Father."[56] Williams' thinking encourages a participatory understanding of the Christian life. The church is of God, and it is of God through Jesus Christ. The emphasis in Acts is on the church of God as witness, witness to God's raising of Jesus and his coming to judge. Witness is the means by which the finite world realizes "the character of quality of the *infinite* reality which is the Word's loving dependence on the Father." We bear witness, then, and we share by the powerful working of the Spirit *in* the benefits of the Son. Those benefits—for example forgiveness—give rise to a sharing in the character of divinity. The direction is from God to us, through Christ, by the power of the Spirit. Accordingly, the church neither realizes nor actualizes anything with respect to God. The church's being is receptive, from beginning to end. It is of God, realizing in the world the infinite reality in which it shares. This is not only true on the level of agency, but it is also true on the level of being. Yes, the agency—the "divine *energia*"—that is in Christ "is an agency that may be shared by other realities."[57] If we think of those other realities in terms of the church, yes, it is right to say that Jesus acts through it, more specifically, that it is a conduit for divine *energia*. It is Jesus who, after all, Paul persecutes; in persecuting believers,

Jesus is persecuted. The church receives divine *energia* through Christ and the benefits conferred. This *energia* is of God.

Further to this, the doctrine of creation has, I think, more work to do than Williams intimates in terms of our thinking about the church of God. The doctrine of creation clarifies not only the absolute difference of God and creatures but also, as Williams rightly avers, "the unconditional freedom of engagement."[58] What makes reading Williams' masterful text odd is that there is not really much of a doctrine of creation. Christology does a lot of work, perhaps all the work, supplanting what a doctrine of creation ought to do, and thus impoverishes what the doctrine of creation contributes to thinking about the church. The doctrine of creation illuminates, for example, the difference between uncreated and created being. It also tells us that God, as the cause of all things, causes them in such a way as to conserve and preserve them in being. Yes, the advent of Christ represents a great intensification of God's engagement with creatures. But that engagement complements a basic metaphysical structure. Creatures are naturally related to their Creator; they share, as creatures, in their Creator's existence. That said, we must always remember that our Creator's existence is not a participated existence. The Creator exists in and of himself.

Christology turns attention toward created things insofar as Jesus effects in the Spirit a radical restoration and intensification of being in relation to God. Christology also issues in an ecclesiology that is of God. I mean by this that it is God's will not so much to pervade, in a wholesale manner, created reality.[59] Rather, God does already pervade things—things are in him. The doctrine of creation infers that. But creatures that exist in relationship to God rarely, because of sin, acknowledge him, let alone love him. Accordingly, God restores the "of"—that the created order, indeed the church, is *of* him and, as a result, must love him. The upshot of this is to not always accord priority to Christology. Christology is of course central, but it is not foundational to either creation or the church. God is. God is the key to Christ and to the church, to say nothing of created things. The task is to state classical themes in a way that does justice to the priority of God, not only in the doctrine of creation but also Christology and ecclesiology.[60]

The church is where—the space wherein—we yield to Christ. "Finite reality is," yes, "supremely itself" in him. And to be in Christ is of course to be in his body, the church. Finite reality is itself in Christ, for he is the one through whom things are. Things are themselves in him because he, in terms of his person (again), is life, for he is from the Father and in the Father. Created things are participations via likeness in the divine life. This life we squelch, trample upon, and resist, all due to sin. Christ, however, is supremely open to and loving of his Father and forms us into a community who is open, too. To be a creature is to imitate Christ and thus to enjoy a greater degree of participation in the life common to him, the Father, and the Spirit. Christ's life shows us what a life from God is like, and the church is the home where such a life takes shape.

Put differently, Jesus Christ is from God, and God speaks in and through Christ. Christ's humiliation is the humiliation of a man who is one with the Father (and always is one with him). Understanding the doctrine of God in self-communicative terms, and Jesus as the culmination of that, is important. However, it cannot displace another even more important idiom, which is participation. Participation has a greater range, applicable to Christology, soteriology, and ecclesiology, but also creation. "Gethsemene and Calvary" do provide clues about "created reality itself in relationship to its maker" but so do created things when considered along participatory lines.[61] Created things are not mute; they are of God, too. All things in their own way answer the question of what God is. I would have liked Williams to say more about that. Acts helps us to see the extent to which the ancestors do not participate in the promise (by and large), turning as they do from the resurrected Christ as fulfillment of the promise. God is not so much "self-gift" in Acts as the one who raises Christ and pours out through him the greatest gift, the Holy Spirit, giving rise to the church.[62] There is in Williams' doctrine of God a constriction of being and act (processions and missions). The unicity of the simple and living God has, I think, much theological work to do, and not just the relations of the persons one to another. This constriction has an impact upon matters downstream, namely creation, Christology, and ecclesiology.

Furthermore, Jesus shows us who God is by his relationship to God, his being the site of God's activity. Jesus is from God, his resurrection is of God, and it is God who judges through him. Jesus shows us what it is to be human by being acted upon, by being entirely transparent to the Father through the Spirit. The key to creatureliness is our origin, God, and our being creatures in whom God sees his own work. The key to Jesus is God's raising of him. "The divine in Christ" is shown by the Father's raising of him.[63] What differentiates Jesus from us is that God does not simply speak and act through him, but that the life of this man is an unceasing participation in God's only begotten Son. This is not so much a "paradox," as Williams avers, but rather the form of the divine Son's processional life among us.[64] The Son of God unites all flesh to himself in the man Jesus. The ministry of Jesus is that of proclaiming a kingdom wherein all may experience and know themselves to be through him, in him, and for him. To be like Jesus is to let ourselves be acted upon by God, to be raised by God through Jesus to new life, and to be a witness to God.

"Metaphysical perspectives" do not simply "*show* themselves."[65] They structure us, as created things, indeed our activity and our experience of ourselves. Acts' "grammar of God" upholds God's supremacy in the strictest sense, whether it be the resurrection, the pouring out of the Spirit, or the church we are considering.[66] God must never be spoken of as being *of* anyone or anything. Everything is of God (the Father): Jesus, the Spirit, the church. An analysis of the 'of' illuminates created things, too. What is of God enjoys a particular kind of participation in God. The 'of' teaches us that created things, including Jesus' own humanity, neither diminish nor compete with God, who is their principle. Instead, for everything to be itself, it must acknowledge its indebtedness to God. Herein Williams is spot-on: doctrine, especially the doctrine of God, is "descriptive and imperative."[67] To live and breathe as if we are really of God, that is our joy and duty. That is the imperative of Acts' relentless theocentrism. In this, we become a little more like Christ, who "understands himself as identical with his work."[68] Our work in this life is to be of God in all things, which is to be like Christ. Christ's origin—his being the eternally begotten Word—is manifest in his work; indeed Jesus is indistinguishable from it. His mission is the temporal expression of his eternal procession. As the Father's only begotten, he is the Savior. But he saves as he does, lives an exemplary life as he does, because of his origin, his being the Father's only Son. We receive the Lord Jesus as this insofar as we listen to, obey, and love him. This is what it means for us to be of God.

Acts' impact upon the systematic enterprise is therefore of great consequence, descriptively and imperatively. We honor God's priority, that all doctrines are derivative of God, the one triune God, Father, Son, and Holy Spirit. We accept, too, that there is a moral, ethical, and ascetic orientation that God's preeminence encourages.

I have endeavored to unfold in this chapter three points of heavenly teaching that warrant systematic reflection in relation to God pursued in an ascetical key. These three points have been referenced throughout the book but not in a terribly sustained and ordered way. Hence the contribution of this penultimate chapter. The witness of Acts to God's raising of Jesus, God's pouring out of the Spirit through Jesus, and God's church show us Acts' preoccupation with God. This is not to exclude Son and Spirit, but it is to show how resurrection, Pentecost, and the church have God (the Father) as their principle. A deep comfort with God as the narrative's main subject and agent does not displace Jesus and the Spirit, but it is to show them as existing and working in a way that is ordered to God. This pattern reflects the procession of Son and Spirit in the divine life. The Spirit's operations are ordered toward

Christ, indeed toward making us partakers in his death and resurrection, and the Son's operation are demonstrative of the Father's authority and priority though not in a way that diminishes his equality with the Father (and Spirit). We conclude by thinking briefly about how Peter's and Paul's temperaments bear upon the treatment of these great themes.

Two Theological Temperaments

These themes are hard to receive without love for God, coming as it does from God. The steadfastness that Peter and Paul exemplify before hostile Jews and Gentiles has, I think, its motor in their love for God. Paul, especially, defers to his testimony, his being spoken to by Christ and being blinded by his light. Paul does so not to draw attention to himself but to show God's determination to take "a people for his name" (Acts 15:18). God looks favorably upon Paul, and Paul testifies to God's having done so in order that the good news may go to the Gentiles. It is worth considering how the narrative sequence of Acts seeds, then, a vision of theology that is in an atmospheric sense both Augustinian and Thomist. Let me explain, and with this I conclude. By that I mean that Paul says a great deal about his previous life, his "believing everything laid down according to the law or written in the prophets" (24:14). Paul does so in order to draw attention to God's raising of Jesus and end-time judgment of all in him. In this respect, Paul is like Augustine, who, as we all know, uses the word "I" quite generously, most obviously in his *Confessions*. Peter, judging by his speeches, tells us nothing about his three years with Jesus. We never hear Peter give his testimony. Peter never so much as alludes to how Jesus appeared to him on the beach, offering him breakfast, asking Peter the most important question ever put to him—"Do you love me?" (cf. John 21:15–19). In this respect, Peter is akin to Thomas, whose teaching and preaching yield no knowledge of the man so doing.

Theology today requires both emphases. There must first be, as with Peter and a contemporary exemplar of Peter's 'style,' someone like the late John Webster (1955–2016), a deep desire "for listeners to hear what the Spirit—rather than John Webster—says to the church."[69] If we think about Webster's (and Peter's) approach in terms of the idiom of nature and grace, Webster's approach is more one of grace either supplanting or displacing nature; Webster's lived experience is unimportant, as it were, in terms of the gospel's declaration. In both volumes of Webster's published sermons, there is, tellingly, not a single reference to the person preaching. That the second half of Acts is essentially the Acts of Paul, and that Paul appeals to his own biography (though not always) before both Jews in Acts 22:1–21 and Gentile rulers like Agrippa in 26:2–23, is significant. In terms of the consequences of this for a systematic presentation of the faith, we, I think, see the import of both. The austere tone that characterizes Thomas (and Calvin) as well as a contemporary exemplar like Webster, indebted though as he is to both, assumes that a vertical preoccupation relegates a horizontal concern in the form of biography, again using Peter as a rough type. The opposite is of course Augustine (and his sixteenth-century student, Luther) insofar as biography is a living feature of their theology, following Paul as a rough type. The devotional character of Augustine's *Confessions* does not belie for a moment its extraordinary doctrinal richness.

The uptake is that Acts honors both, though the weight is, I think, on Paul. Given that Augustine wrote and ministered as a bishop and leader of a monastery, and Thomas as for the most part a university lecturer teaching those aspiring to orders, it would seem that the ecclesial home of Augustine's theology *perhaps* allows you to see features of gospel teaching that a home less open to the autobiographical (the thirteenth-century university) would infer, following again Peter as a rough type. I mean this to suggest that Jesus' preaching, teaching, and enactment of the kingdom of God according to Luke requires Acts for its fulfillment, in particular the proclamation of Paul. Paul of course does not preach himself but "Christ crucified" (Gal 2:20). That said, Paul's preaching has the impact that it does because Paul's experience is front and center in a way that it is not in Peter. Theology needs both temperaments. However, a move from Peter (with Thomas as a rough type) to Paul (with Augustine in the mode of the *Confessions* as a rough type) is salutary. In keeping with this, the end of Luke-Acts provides profound instruction for the Christian today and points to the disposition that the church catholic in our later modern globalized world should assume.

Christians live, like Paul, at their own expense. The magistrates are not paying for them to be there. The leaders of Christian communities welcome all who come through their doors, whether they be disciples or whether they bear more of a resemblance to the crowds, who are always objects of Jesus' compassion. Leadership in continuity with the apostles (especially Paul) welcomes all. Remember that those whom Paul welcomes in Rome are Jews, "the brothers" (Acts 28:21). Paul knows that his own people need to hear gospel teaching about the Lord Jesus, not only for their sake but for the Gentiles as well. Paul welcomes them, proclaiming the good news to them, all the while knowing that while some are convinced, many others refuse to believe. This would seem to characterize many congregations today. Why does Paul bother with them, aside from the fact that they are those who come to see him? Because the uneven and mixed reception of "the brothers" is the occasion for the sending of God's salvation to the Gentiles.

Contemporary congregational leadership need not be alarmed at the mixed reception of the gospel among those gathered. Why? Because God uses without condoning what is lukewarm to occasion the faithful's going forth to fields ripe for harvest, fields full of those who listen. The profoundly mixed character of the church of God—wheat and tares coexisting side by side—has a specific purpose in God's economy. Indeed, it serves as the motivation to proclaim to those who have not yet heard. Why? To arouse those who think they have heard so they might hear afresh, and to fall once more in love with God.

In order to encourage love for God, both temperaments are necessary, that is, Peter's (with Thomas as an inheritor) and Paul's (with Augustine as exemplar). It is okay for a serious systematic presentation of the faith to proceed in an at times experientially laden way.[70] Even then, however, the I is surrounded by the what and the who of God. The what and who of God is far more interesting, demanding, and salutary than the I. But again, there is no competition, for theology attends to the thrice-holy God—the great I Am—relating all things to this God. Theology relates the I to God. Each one of us may now be seen only in relationship to the resurrected Son of God, the Spirit poured out from God through the one appointed by God to judge all before God, and to the church of God as it proclaims to fields ripe for harvest the salvation of God.

Conclusion

God is theology's source and end. Without God, there would be nothing. And yet, there is, of course, something. The something that God gifts us with and that we have considered in this study is Scripture, specifically the Acts of the Apostles. We attended to it as a sign, a great gift that communicates God's desire to be served and loved, among both Jews and Gentiles, as the one who raised Jesus and poured out his Spirit through him. We have been mindful throughout of the priority apostolic preaching ascribes to God. We have endeavored to look at principal teachings constituting something of the substance of the faith from the vantage point of God. We have an apostolic gospel to proclaim because of God. It is God's message. The message unsettles and overturns many cherished convictions, especially in regard to the range of the forgiveness of sins. We see that Israel's pardon and restoration involve the inclusion of the Gentiles. At the same time, the text of Acts does not simply disrupt. It also confirms. What does it confirm? It shows the earth to be the object of and indeed participant in God's lovingkindness and care. The earth that is the Lord's shares in what he is. It is and remains good. And its goodness is seen (in part) by a structural truth. I have written about created things in relationship to God. I think that understanding created things as participations is the most fitting way in which to account for the nature of creatureliness. The Creator makes things in such a way that they search for their Creator. The hunger that God-fearing Gentiles such as Cornelius experience in relationship to Israel's God has to do with how we are made. We are created by God and for God. Our innocence and original desire for God have of course been shattered by our embrace of our first parents' sin. Sin is not ignorance, but ignorance is something of sin's form. The response that apostolic proclamation elicits is repentance, a turn from our willful ignorance. The announcement of the news that God raised Jesus and will judge all through him "in righteousness" demands repentance (Acts 17:31) from sin and ignorance that enslaves.

The text of Acts (as with the text of Scripture), because its author is God, encourages us to contemplate it with respect to God and with respect to what is required of us in light of what it says about God. This is a matter of twofold theological responsibility. First, theological responsibility entails God, loving attention to this One. The message spoken so boldly would not be without God and obedience to him. Second, this message relates all things to God. Things that one might have thought were only tangentially related to Israel's God, most especially Gentiles, are seen in light of God's raising of Jesus to be objects of divine mercy, recipients of the grace of the Lord Jesus, and receptive to the signs and wonders of the Spirit. Theological responsibility also entails becoming a certain sort of person before God, a person who loves God and is eager to hear the word of God through his apostolic emissaries.

This pursuit of such a task, structured as something of a listening exercise, has also sought to make an intervention in and contribution toward contemporary systematic theology. I have drawn upon a more participatory account of the God/world relation so as to show where shortcomings and certain strengths lie in the work of Kathrine Sonderegger and Rowan Williams. Far from being a contribution to international Calvin scholarship, I have used Calvin so as to help me to listen to Peter and Paul speak and preach. I have then drawn upon others such as Augustine and Thomas to help me synthesize and order what Calvin thinks Peter and Paul are saying about God and us in relation to God. Acts raises, moreover, and in quite stark terms, theology's purpose and end as well as its beginning. Theology does not begin in a space devoid of God, his life-giving speech and presence. Theology begins with repentance, with the acknowledgment that all human undertaking (theology included) expresses rejection of the "Holy and Righteous One" and he who sends this one (Acts 3:14). Theology proceeds before the God whom we would rather reject, whose reality we are happy to have usurped by our own ignorance, in whose being we would really rather not participate. Yes, this is something of theology's temperament: a repentant one. And yet, what always surrounds our idolatrous and murderous hearts is a great promise, "the promise of the Father," the Father who is also our loving Creator (1:4). Theology proceeds under the promise that the one who creates and sustains us in being will perfect us in the end via his Word and Spirit. Acts' blunt and sobering description of the human condition is made possible by the promising God who is never without witness to himself.[1]

God's rule, his kingdom, stands as Calvin argues at the center of Jesus' preaching and indeed of the theological enterprise. What is at the center is of God. Accordingly, we describe God's rule inasmuch as we repent before God. Repentance is the form his rule takes among us, its content being God. Theology's business is to learn from Peter and Paul, drawing attention to the attributes of God and of how this God sends the promised Spirit, having lifted Jesus up to heaven. Theology takes its time with this God, seeing how everything Acts says in relationship to Jesus and the Spirit, to say nothing of Peter's and Paul's preaching and teaching ministry, is of God. This enables us to see how and to live as if everything may be said to be related to God.

Even Paul's testimony illuminates this pattern. Saul's zeal for God is not, initially, leavened by a knowledge of God's will, which is that Saul would see and hear "the righteous one" (Acts 3:14). Saul, of course, does come to hear, becoming Paul in the process. Zeal for God must be perfected by sight and by hearing of the Savior, as Paul's testimony indicates. Such theology, too, in its zeal for divine things must see and hear of this Jesus who is of God. Theology helps equip the church to witness to God in accordance with his will, which is that we would see and hear Jesus. We see Jesus with the eyes of our heart as we listen to him speak to us in the Spirit through the Scriptures.

If Scripture is theology's source, its ongoing food, and its perennial delight, then there is a strong argument to be made for pursuing the systematic task in an almost commentarial mode. The vast majority of us will never be able to see things in a systematic way with the perspicuity of a Thomas, for example, but we can see how many of the things about which he wrote in his more summative works have scriptural salience. Theology's form is fundamentally scriptural. Every once in a while, someone will arise with the intellectual and spiritual gifts necessary to present an ordered account of the whole. But for most of us who are called to a vocation in theology, we will be content pursuing what Katherine Sonderegger calls "spiritual exegesis."[2] We listen in the Spirit to what God says through the One whom he raised, passing on the fruits of our hearing through pulpit, care of souls, the classroom and videoconference suite, to say nothing of the scholarly page. Accordingly, theology's remit takes a humble form. Hear this God speak; repent before him; and as we wait for the Savior to come again to judge, we bear witness to what we have seen with the eyes of the heart and heard with ears cleansed by baptismal waters. When theology is pursued in an explicitly scriptural idiom and voice, then its testing function in relation to the church's preaching also becomes clear. Is the church preaching a gospel of its own devising, or is it bearing witness to the gospel, testifying to God's kingdom? Is what the church preaches recognizable, scripturally speaking?

In conclusion, we turn for a moment to Paul. When Paul defends himself before the council in Acts 23:1–11, he, in a fit of anger, insults a man who he does not realize is "the high priest" (23:5). In a move of extraordinary brilliance, Paul says that he did not "realize, brothers, that he was high priest" (23:5). But what Paul does not say—which is what the "brothers" say—is that he is "God's high priest" (23:4). The high priest's inability to hear Jesus through the ancestral law and the prophetic speech means that he is not "*God's* high priest," only instead "high priest" (emphasis mine). The high priest misjudges as he does because he is not of God; he is not, to use a Johannine idiom, born again. Were he of God, he would receive Paul's witness to "the hope of the resurrection of the dead" (23:6).

There is a lesson here for theology. Theology's vocation is to be of God. To be of God is to be of the Scriptures, to see and hear in them the message of Jesus raised as God's eschatological judge. To see and hear as such is to see and hear in the Spirit of God and to relate all that is seen to God. Insofar as we do so, the baptized fulfill the call to be of God in all that is said and done. The message of the speeches is utterly and profoundly relevant to theology: to trace how the kingdom of God is *of* God; to show that were it not for God, there would be *no*thing: no ancestral law, no prophetic voices calling for obedience to it; no fulfillment of the promise in a way inclusive of Gentiles; and no eschatological manifestation of Christ as judge. The lesson for theology and for the life of the saints is quite simple: to be, recognizably, *of* God.

Notes

Introduction

1   Augustine of Hippo, *Confessions*, trans. Henry Chadwick (Oxford: Oxford University Press, 1991), 3.5.

2   Jean Calvin, *Commentary on Acts*, 6:19. All citations of Calvin's commentary on Acts use the English translation of David Torrance and Thomas Torrance. See *Calvin's New Testament Commentaries*, vol. 6, *Acts 1–13*, ed. David W. Torrance and Thomas F. Torrance (Grand Rapids: Eerdmans, 1994); *Calvin's New Testament Commentaries*, vol. 7, *Acts 14–28*, ed. David W. Torrance and Thomas F. Torrance (Grand Rapids: Eerdmans, 1994).

3   Calvin, *Commentary on Acts*, 6:130.

4   I will make reference to Stephen's wonderful speech in Acts 7 in treating Peter's speeches in part 1; the same is true with James' speech in 15:13–21.

5   Calvin, *Commentary on Acts*, 6:19.

6   See Calvin, *Commentary on Acts*, 6:79. Calvin says of Peter's second speech in 2:14–36, his Pentecost speech, that "we have therefore in these few words almost the sum total of Christianity."

7   Calvin, *Commentary on Acts*, 6:3.

8   Peter's eight speeches are found in 1:16–22; 2:14–26; 3:12–26; 4:8–12; 5:29–32; 10:34–43; 11:5–17; and 15:7–11. With the exception of Paul's first speech in 13:16–41, the rest of his speeches are located in the second half of the book, namely

in 17:22–31; 20:18–35; 22:1–21; 24:10–21; 26:2–23; and 28:17–20, 26–28.

9 Calvin, *Commentary on Acts*, 6:3.

10 Calvin, *Commentary on Acts*, 6:4.

11 Katherine Sonderegger, *Systematic Theology*, vol. 1, *The Doctrine of God* (Minneapolis: Fortress, 2015); *Systematic Theology*, vol. 2, *The Doctrine of the Holy Trinity: Processions and Persons* (Minneapolis: Fortress, 2020).

12 Sonderegger, *Systematic Theology*, 1:82.

13 See, for example, Sonderegger, *Systematic Theology*, 1:391, 2:379.

14 See further the recent and masterful work of Andrew Davison, titled *Participation in God*. I draw from Davison from time to time in this study. Davison, *Participation in God: A Study in Christian Doctrine and Metaphysics* (Cambridge: Cambridge University Press, 2019).

15 Rowan Williams, *Christ the Heart of Creation* (London: Continuum, 2018), 233.

16 Williams, *Christ*, 6.

17 Oliver O'Donovan, *Ethics as Theology*, vol. 1, *Self, World, and Time* (Grand Rapids: Eerdmans, 2013), 57. The second volume is titled *Finding and Seeking* (Grand Rapids: Eerdmans, 2014), the third *Entering into Rest* (Grand Rapids: Eerdmans, 2017).

18 Calvin's two-volume commentary appeared in two parts, the first part in 1552, the second in 1554. As Wilhelmus H. Th. Moehn puts it in his important chapter, Calvin "preached in the Genevan congregation on Acts during the same period that he was writing his commentary. In the scope of his entire exegetical work, this close coincidence between his sermons and his commentary on the same part of Scripture is unique." See Moehn, "Calvin as Commentator on the Acts of the Apostles," in *Calvin and the Bible*, ed. Donald K. McKim (Cambridge: Cambridge University Press, 2006), 199; as well as Christopher R. J. Holmes, "What Does Calvin's Engagement with Acts Teach Us about God's Providence?" *Journal of Reformed Theology* 15 (2021): 208–24.

19 Eric L. Mascall, *The Triune God: An Ecumenical Study* (Allison Park, Penn.: Pickwick, 1986), 8.

20   The work of, for example, Janusz Kucicki is the kind of bib-
      lical work that I have little interest in encouraging. Though I
      have read his monograph, I find the genre of modern biblical
      criticism, at least as he instantiates it, rather suffocating. I am
      interested in what the text compels us to think, do, and say, not
      simply in what it said. I treat the text as the living word of the
      Lord. See Janusz Kucicki, *The Function of the Speeches in the Acts
      of the Apostles: A Key to Interpretation of Luke's Use of Speeches
      in Acts* (Leiden: Brill, 2018). Furthermore, I have decided, in
      the interests of promoting an exegetically disciplined and theo-
      centric account of the faith, to engage in an ongoing conversa-
      tion within the book's footnotes. That conversation is with Luke
      Timothy Johnson, the well-known and respected lay Roman
      Catholic biblical scholar of Luke-Acts. Johnson is useful because
      he receives Luke-Acts as the word of God for the people of God,
      but he does so in a way that is far too constrained by modern
      interpretive conventions. As shall be seen, the chief convention
      that I resist is Johnson's conviction that it is "Luke's *depiction*
      [emphasis mine] of the church" that we encounter in Acts. Such
      a way of framing things puts, as we shall see, too much empha-
      sis on Luke's agency and not enough on God's. See Johnson,
      *Prophetic Jesus, Prophetic Church: The Challenge of Luke-Acts
      to Contemporary Christians* (Grand Rapids: Eerdmans, 2011), x
      (hereafter cited as *PJPC*).

21   Hans Boersma, *Seeing God: The Beatific Vision in Christian Tra-
      dition* (Grand Rapids: Eerdmans, 2018), 276.

22   Calvin, *Commentary on Acts*, 6:79.

23   Johnson's enthusiasm for thinking about Luke as an author
      in naturalistic terms is strong, making it difficult to engage in
      what I call a listening exercise. A revealing passage runs: "Luke
      constructs the character of Jesus and the early church in accord
      with what he understood Jesus' prophetic message to have
      been. I do not mean to suggest that there was no basis in real-
      ity for his portrait, but only that his portrait isolates and devel-
      ops those tracts that form an embodiment of the prophetic
      word" (*PJPC*, 123). I think it wise to acknowledge that Luke's
      portrait develops not only what Luke thinks is important but

also that Luke develops as he does because of the sanctifying and directive work of the Spirit. Johnson does not seem "to accord the spiritual dimension of things any reality of its own." Though Bentley Hart says this of science, it is equally true of a certain strand of New Testament scholarship as evidenced by Johnson. See Hart's essay "Should Science Think?" in *Theological Territories: A David Bentley Hart Digest* (Notre Dame, Ind.: University of Notre Dame Press, 2020), 150. Johnson's naturalism, moreover, leads him to say that Luke's vision is "a utopian vision for the church" (*PJPC*, 123). That, I think, is simply unhelpful. Luke's vision attests, instead, the spread through the Mediterranean world of the good news of the kingdom as including Jews and Gentiles.

1 The Mercy of God

1   I take issue with Johnson's characterization of theology as "both inductive and nonsystematic." Theology, thus conceived, is "necessarily revisionist." Johnson continues, "Luke shows how new insight into God derives from actual human experience" (*PJPC*, 69). That is well and good; however, it is unhelpful to juxtapose "ecclesial tradition" and "the push of prophetic voices" (*PJPC*, 71). Instead, I think it better to argue that the dogma of the church establishes "certain boundaries" while also invariably opening "up entire new vistas." I am indebted to David Bentley Hart for this insight. See Hart, "Tradition and Authority: A Vaguely Gnostic Meditation," in Hart, *Theological Territories*, 107.

2   Calvin, *Commentary on Acts*, 6:24.

3   Calvin, *Commentary on Acts*, 6:31.

4   Calvin, *Commentary on Acts*, 6:51.

5   Aquinas, *ST* 1.21.3. I use the version from Anton C. Pegis throughout the work for the *prima pars*, *prima-secunda pars*, and *secunda-secundae pars*, and the Cambridge Black Friars version for the *tertia pars*. See Aquinas, *Basic Writings of Saint Thomas Aquinas*, ed. Anton C. Pegis (New York: Random House, 1945); idem, *Summa Theologiae*, trans. Blackfriars (Cambridge: Cambridge University Press, 1964).

6   Aquinas, *ST* 1.21.3.

7   John Webster, "Mercy," in *God without Measure: Working Papers in Christian Theology*, vol. 2, *Virtue and Intellect* (London: T&T Clark, 2015), 54.

8   Aquinas, *ST* 1.19.2.

9   Calvin, *Commentary on Acts*, 6:51.

10   Calvin, *Commentary on Acts*, 6:32.

11   My biggest objection to Johnson's approach is its romantic and rather domesticated impulse. Johnson writes of Luke-Acts that it *"imagines* [emphasis mine] a world that challenges the one that humans in every age construct on their own terms" (*PJPC*, vii). Acts of course perennially challenges idols, but it does so because of God. The notion that Luke "imagines" domesticates God's involvement with Luke's text acquiring the shape and content that it does. In short, Luke's text is inspired, meaning that our sense of what Acts is as sacred Scripture must be related first and foremost to God. Acts, as written by Luke, is God's instrument for communicating apostolic proclamation. Luke's authorial mind displays a watertight orientation toward God. This orientation is reflected in the Godward direction of his writing. As David Bentley Hart writes of phenomena in general, "No phenomenon proceeds from itself alone, at least not if it really is a *phenomenon.*" This is certainly true of that most sacred phenomenon, Holy Scripture. See Hart, "Remarks Made to Jean-Luc Marion regarding Revelation and Givenness," in Hart, *Theological Territories*, 41.

12   Calvin, *Commentary on Acts*, 6:63.

13   Aquinas, *ST* 1.105.4, ad3.

14   See further Matthew Levering, *Predestination: Biblical and Theological Paths* (Oxford: Oxford University Press, 2011), 29, n. 39.

15   David Fergusson, *The Providence of God: A Polyphonic Approach* (Cambridge: Cambridge University Press, 2019), 231. As Levering notes of Augustine and Aquinas, "one finds an emphasis on the transcendent causality of God acting (by nature and by grace) in and through the human free will." See Levering, *Predestination*, 116.

16   Aquinas, *ST* 1.21.3, ad2.

17   Aquinas, *ST* 1.21.3.

18   Calvin, *Commentary on Acts*, 6:61.

19   Ulrich Zwingli, *On Providence and Other Essays*, trans. William John Hinke (Eugene, Oreg.: Wipf and Stock, 1999), 185–86.

20   Cf. Webster, "Mercy," 56: "His [God's] 'apathy', his freedom from destructive passion, is not a protection against mercy but the energy with which his mercy is exercised and which makes it truly capable of meeting the creature's need."

21   Calvin, *Commentary on Acts*, 6:64.

22   Aquinas, *ST* 1.21.3.

23   The agency ascribed to the church in Johnson's account is an issue too. Johnson writes "that the church continues the healing ministry of Jesus" (*PJPC*, 147). Such a description undervalues the ongoing agency and contemporaneity of Jesus' ministry in the Spirit. Accordingly, the church does not so much continue his "healing ministry" but participate or share in it. Very often, the church, taking its cues from Israel's own history, obscures the promise and thus God's desire to manifest and glorify himself before the nations. Indeed, God very often contradicts and overturns his own people's insouciance in fulfilling the covenant. It is good, then, to put a bit more space between Jesus and the church—the church as witness to and participant in Jesus' ministry of restoration.

24   Aquinas, *ST* 1.25.3, ad3.

25   Aquinas, *ST* 1.25.3.

26   Aquinas, *ST* 1.25.4, ad3.

27   Aquinas, *ST* 1.25.1, ad3.

28   Aquinas, *ST* 1.25.1.

29   Aquinas, *ST* 1.25.3, ad3.

30   Aquinas, *ST* 1.105.2.

31   Aquinas, *ST* 1.103.4.

32   Aquinas, *ST* 1.104.4.

33   Aquinas, *ST* 1.103.4.

34   Aquinas, *ST* 1.103.1.

35   Aquinas, *ST* 1.104.3, ad1.

36   Aquinas, *ST* 1.104.3, ad1.

37 Aquinas, *ST* 1.105.4.

38 Aquinas, *ST* 1.103.7, ad3.

39 Aquinas, *ST* 1.21.3.

40 Aquinas, *ST* 1.23.1, ad3.

41 Jean Calvin, *Institutes of the Christian Religion*, trans. Ford Lewis Battles (Philadelphia: Westminster, 1960), 1.17.1. The words "determination," "decree," and "will" seem to be synonymous in Calvin's account.

42 The full note runs: God's "decree" is a matter of God's "concern for the whole human race, but especially his vigilance in ruling the church." See Calvin, *Institutes*, 1.17.1. Calvin's emphasis on God raises a point similar to the objection raised in n. 32 with respect to Johnson insofar as Johnson places too much emphasis on the church's agency. Johnson argues that the church "can continue and extend Jesus' prophetic work in the world" (*PJPC*, vii). I would rather that Johnson emphasize Jesus' agency. The church does not "continue and extend" Jesus' prophetic work in the world. The church, instead, witnesses to Jesus, whom God raised as present and active in the Spirit, drawing men and women to himself through apostolic preaching. Too much emphasis is, in Jesus' account, placed on the church, and not enough on Jesus, whom God raised, and who is exalted and glorified and continues, at the Father's behest, to invigorate and suffuse the preaching of the gospel.

43 Church of England, *The Book of Common Prayer: 1662 Version (Includes Appendices from the 1549 Version and Other Commemorations)* (London: David Campbell, 1999).

44 Calvin, *Commentary on Acts*, 6:125.

45 Calvin, *Commentary on Acts*, 6:139.

46 Calvin, *Commentary on Acts*, 6:141. This notion of Israel's history as a disaster is Jenson's. See Robert W. Jenson, *Ezekiel* (Grand Rapids: Brazos, 2009), 154.

47 Calvin, *Commentary on Acts*, 6:149.

48 Calvin, *Commentary on Acts*, 6:150.

49 Calvin, *Commentary on Acts*, 6:153.

50 Jenson, *Ezekiel*, 154.

51   Jaroslav Pelikan, *Commentary on Acts* (Grand Rapids: Brazos, 2005), 70.

52   Augustine of Hippo, *Confessions*, 1.4.

53   Aquinas, *ST* 1.25.1, ad3. Thomas also can say that the principle of creation is the processions of the divine persons. See Aquinas, *ST* 1.45.6, ad1.

54   Pelikan, *Commentary on Acts*, 70.

55   Calvin, *Commentary on Acts*, 6:308.

56   Calvin, *Commentary on Acts*, 6:190.

57   Sonderegger, *Systematic Theology*, 1:236.

58   Sonderegger, *Systematic Theology*, 1:330.

59   Sonderegger, *Systematic Theology*, 1:321.

60   See Sonderegger, *Systematic Theology*, 1:434.

61   Sonderegger, *Systematic Theology*, 2:277. Emphasis is original throughout unless otherwise noted.

62   Sonderegger, *Systematic Theology*, 2:383.

63   Williams, *Christ*, 225. Erich Przywara is background here. See further Przywara, *Analogia Entis: Metaphysics; Original Structure and Universal Rhythm* (Grand Rapids: Eerdmans, 2014).

64   Williams, *Christ*, 228.

65   Calvin, *Commentary on Acts*, 6:306.

66   Calvin, *Commentary on Acts*, 6:300.

67   Calvin, *Commentary on Acts*, 6:309.

68   Webster, "Mercy," 55.

69   Calvin, *Commentary on Acts*, 6:230.

70   Calvin, *Commentary on Acts*, 6:278.

71   Cf. Thomas in Aquinas, *ST* 1.19.3, ad2: "Although God necessarily wills His own goodness, He does not necessarily will things willed on account of His goodness; for it can exist without other things."

72   Calvin, *Commentary on Acts*, 6:305.

73   Aquinas, *ST* 1.21.4.

74   Aquinas, *ST* 1.21.4, ad2.

75   Aquinas, *ST* 1.21.3, ad2.

76   Calvin, *Commentary on Acts*, 6:322.

77 Karl Barth, *Church Dogmatics*, ed. George W. Bromiley and Thomas F. Torrance (Edinburgh: T&T Clark, 1957–1969), III/3, 207.

78 Though Calvin says this of Paul and Silas on the basis of Acts 15:32, the judgment is equally true of Peter. See Calvin, *Commentary on Acts*, 7:58.

79 Aquinas, *ST* 1.21.8, ad2.

80 Aquinas, *ST* 1.21.4.

2 The Grace of Christ

1 Johnson's description of the rule or kingdom of God in relation to Jesus is a bit strained. Johnson writes of Jesus that his "actions flow from his character and serve the cause of making the rule of God present and effective" (*PJPC*, 133). Jesus does not so much make God's rule "effective" as proclaim that God's rule is, in him, present and effective. All that Jesus does and says is because of his filial relationship to the Father; Jesus' words and deeds are expressive of and receive their principle of intelligibility in relationship to the Father. What Jesus says and does participates in God's rule and presents it.

2 The language of "pattern," "nature," "state," and "condition" comes from Calvin. See Calvin, *Commentary on Acts*, 6:3.

3 See Aquinas, *ST* 1–2.110.1, resp.

4 Calvin, *Commentary on Acts*, 6:17.

5 Calvin, *Commentary on Acts*, 6:18.

6 See, e.g., 1:22; 2:32; 5:32.

7 Calvin, *Commentary on Acts*, 6:35.

8 See further Calvin, *Commentary on Acts*, 6:35.

9 See Aquinas, *ST* 1–2.110.1.

10 Calvin, *Commentary on Acts*, 6:57.

11 Calvin, *Commentary on Acts*, 6:67.

12 Calvin, *Commentary on Acts*, 6:73.

13 See further Brendon Crowe's work *The Hope of Israel: The Resurrection of Christ in the Acts of the Apostles* (Grand Rapids: Baker Academic, 2020).

14 Calvin, *Commentary on Acts*, 6:73.

15 See for example Luke 9:43. Though Jesus heals the boy with the demon, it is God who is praised.

16 Calvin, *Commentary on Acts*, 6:73.

17 Williams, *Christ*, 220.

18 Williams, *Christ*, 131.

19 Williams, *Christ*, 221.

20 See Aquinas, *ST* 1.34.3.

21 Davison, *Participation*, 53.

22 This is Augustine's locution. See book 5 of *De Trinitate*. Augustine of Hippo, *The Trinity*, trans. Edmund Hill (Brooklyn: New City Press, 1997).

23 See further Williams, *Christ*, 246.

24 Sonderegger, *Systematic Theology*, 2:6.

25 See further Sonderegger, *Systematic Theology*, 2:552.

26 Sonderegger, *Systematic Theology*, 2:431.

27 Sonderegger, *Systematic Theology*, 2:457.

28 Sonderegger, *Systematic Theology*, 2:469.

29 Isa 53:3; Sonderegger, *Systematic Theology*, 2:314.

30 Sonderegger, *Systematic Theology*, 2:466.

31 Augustine of Hippo, *Trinity*, 2.1.3.

32 Augustine of Hippo, *Trinity*, 2.1.3.

33 Augustine of Hippo, *Trinity*, 2.1.4; Calvin, *Commentary on Acts*, 6:73. Some texts, moreover, refer neither to his equality with the Father nor to his being "according to the flesh" but rather "simply to his being." That said, Augustine writes little about the third notion.

34 Augustine of Hippo, *Trinity*, 2.1.3.

35 Augustine of Hippo, *Trinity*, 2.1.4.

36 Augustine of Hippo, *Trinity*, 2.1.4.

37 Calvin, *Commentary on Acts*, 6:73.

38 I do not know what Johnson means when he says that Luke "portrays Jesus as a public figure" (*PJPC*, 169). While the 'Messianic secret' motif is not operative in Luke as it is in Mark, Jesus is no less public and indeed visible in Mark. The difference between Luke and Mark is that Mark ties Jesus' visibility more explicitly to the cross, though to describe this difference by suggesting it amounts to different authorial perspectives diminishes the work

of the Spirit in commandeering their authorial voices so that the shape of their Gospels reflects God's intention. Johnson would, I think, concur with what I have said. My point is that the agency of Luke, the author, seems to display that of God. There need not be tension between the two. There is, rather, continuity under two different modes, the divine and the human. There is not any competition between the two, though the human is ordered to the divine. The divine voice is the principal of the human (authorial) voice, and there is consonance between them.

39 This is from editorial note a, p. 7, Aquinas, *ST* 3.7.1. This note is supplied by the Dominican translators of the volume.

40 See Acts 3:1–10.

41 Aquinas, *ST* 3.7.1.

42 Aquinas, *ST* 3.7.1, ad1. Note that Thomas uses this language with respect to Christ's soul.

43 See above in the notes for this chapter.

44 Thomas F. O'Meara, "Grace as a Theological Structure in the 'Summa theologiae' of Thomas Aquinas," *Recherches de Théologie Ancienne et Médiévale* 55 (1988): 146. Or, as Michael Gorman argues, it "is enough to allow us to say that the two natures are united in person but not in nature." See Gorman, *Aquinas on the Metaphysics of the Hypostatic Union* (Cambridge: Cambridge University Press, 2017), 51.

45 Aquinas, *ST* 3.7.1, ad1.

46 Aquinas, *ST* 3.7.1, ad3.

47 Aquinas, *ST* 3.7.12, ad2.

48 Aquinas, *ST* 3.7.1, ad2.

49 Aquinas, *ST* 3.7.1, ad1.

50 See Augustine of Hippo, *Trinity*, 2.1.

51 Aquinas, *ST* 3.7.4.

52 Aquinas, *ST* 3.7.5.

53 Aquinas, *ST* 3.7.5.

54 Aquinas, *ST* 3.7.5, ad2.

55 Matthew Wilcoxen, *Divine Humility: God's Morally Perfect Being* (Waco, Tex.: Baylor University Press, 2019), 133.

56 Aquinas, *ST* 3.7.12, ad2.

57 Calvin, *Commentary on Acts*, 6:128.

58 Aquinas, *ST* 3.7.7, ad1.

59 Aquinas, *ST* 3.7.7, ad1.

60 Aquinas, *ST* 3.7.7, ad2.

61 Aquinas, *ST* 3.7.9.

62 Aquinas, *ST* 3.7.10.

63 Gal 4:4; Aquinas, *ST* 3.7.10, ad3.

64 Aquinas, *ST* 3.7.11, resp.

65 Aquinas, *ST* 3.7.11, ad1.

66 Aquinas, *ST* 3.7.12.

67 Aquinas, *ST* 3.7.12, ad2.

68 Aquinas, *ST* 3.7.11, resp.

69 Notice the direction: humanity is always on the receiving end.

70 Calvin, *Commentary on Acts*, 6:299.

71 Calvin, *Commentary on Acts*, 6:311.

72 Calvin, *Commentary on Acts*, 6:149.

73 Calvin, *Commentary on Acts*, 7:35.

74 Calvin, *Commentary on Acts*, 7:41.

75 Calvin, *Commentary on Acts*, 7:93.

76 Calvin, *Commentary on Acts*, 7:94.

77 The sharp divide that Johnson posits between Jesus and Israel's prophetic tradition is overdone. Johnson writes, "Jesus' ministry of embrace should in fact shock, since it so clearly flies in the face of all precedent for Reform within Israel and the prophetic tradition" (*PJPC*, 145). I do not see how Jesus' words and deeds fly in the face of earlier prophetic reform, given how often he cites the prophets with a view to his continuity within them. The church too expands a new thing but one that is by no means discontinuous with Israel. Instead, the people of God are expanded so as to include Gentiles, the very fulfillment of the prophetic sense that the nations will one day be drawn to worship of Israel's God, the one true God.

78 Calvin, *Commentary on Acts*, 7:36.

79 Calvin, *Commentary on Acts*, 7:236.

80 Calvin, *Commentary on Acts*, 6:127.

3 The Hope of the Spirit

1 Calvin, *Commentary on Acts*, 6:19.

2 John Webster, "Principles of Systematic Theology," in *The Domain of the Word: Scripture and Theological Reason* (London: T&T Clark,

2012), 143; "Love" and "Gift" are what Thomas calls "proper" and "personal" names for the Holy Spirit. See Aquinas, *ST* 1.37.1, resp.; 1.38.1, resp. The Son does cause the Spirit but in a mediate way. The Spirit proceeds from the Father—immediately—and through the Son—mediately. For a detailed account of the Spirit's person along broadly Thomistic lines, see my chapter in "The Procession of the Spirit: Eternal Spiration," in *The Orthodox Doctrine of the Trinity: What's at Stake in Recent Debates*, ed. Matthew Barrett (Downers Grove, Ill.: IVP Academic, 2022).

3 Calvin, *Commentary on Acts*, 6:20.

4 Willie James Jennings' very helpful work on Acts errs at just this point. Jennings writes that "there is only one central character in this story of Acts. It is God, the Holy Spirit." See Jennings, *Acts* (Louisville, Ky.: Westminster John Knox, 2017), 2. I think it is better simply to say God, that is, "It is God"—full stop as it were.

5 Calvin, *Commentary on Acts*, 6:57.

6 Johnson is to be applauded for drawing attention to the Spirit as the creative and disclosive power of God. What is unnerving, however, is his description of the Spirit "as the symbol for the living God." See *PJPC*, 66. Such language falls dramatically short of Nicene and Constantinopolitan descriptions of the Spirit as the "Lord and life-giver." Indeed, if the Spirit is only a "symbol," then the nature of salvation is jeopardized. See *PJPC*, 69. In this regard, David Bentley Hart writes, "And if, in the sacraments of the church and the life of sanctification, it is the Spirit who joins us to the Son, and only God can join us to God, then the Spirit too must be God in this wholly consubstantial sense." See Hart, "Tradition and Authority," 114.

7 Mascall, *Triune God*, 36.

8 Mascall, *Triune God*, 37.

9 Jennings, *Acts*, 34.

10 Calvin, *Commentary on Acts*, 6:131.

11 Calvin, *Commentary on Acts*, 6:138.

12 Jennings, *Acts*, 36.

13 Calvin, *Commentary on Acts*, 6:155.

14 Calvin, *Commentary on Acts*, 6:169.

15 Calvin, *Commentary on Acts*, 6:163.

16 So Gal 6:2: "Bear one another's burdens, and in this way you will fulfill the law of Christ."

17 Cf. Luke 24:27: "Then beginning with Moses and all the prophets, he interpreted to them the things about himself in all the scriptures."

18 Calvin, *Commentary on Acts*, 6:318.

19 Jennings, *Acts*, 8.

20 Basil of Caesarea, *On the Holy Spirit*, trans. Stephen Hildebrand (Yonkers, N.Y.: St. Vladimir's Seminary Press, 2011), 1.2.

21 Basil, *On the Holy Spirit*, 9.23.

22 Calvin, *Commentary on Acts*, 6:179.

23 Calvin, *Commentary on Acts*, 6:209.

24 This way of putting things is indebted to Mascall. "St Augustine's adoption of the category of relation and his elevation of it to the level of substance is, of course, an example, perhaps the supreme example, of the use of analogy in theology." *Triune God*, 18.

25 See Mascall, *Triune God*, 37.

26 The Son is present too, though in a different way, mainly in the form of the angel of the Lord.

27 Mascall, *Triune God*, 36.

28 Mascall, *Triune God*, 40 (emphasis in original).

29 This is Thomas' language. See Aquinas, *ST* 1.37.1, ad4.

30 Calvin, *Commentary on Acts*, 6:177.

31 Jennings writes, "The space of Israel is expanding by the Spirit and the number of people who worship the God of Israel is growing." See *Acts*, 8.

32 The language is Calvin's (*Commentary on Acts*, 3:24).

33 Jennings, *Acts*, 110, 142.

34 Kucicki, *Acts*, 348.

35 Jenson, *Ezekiel*, 154.

36 What is salutary in Johnson's account is his reminder of just how "shocking, even outrageous, [is the] character of the initiative that dominates the entire second half of Luke's second volume" (*PJPC*, 152). Yes, it is shocking that in the narrative of Acts, the gospel, the preaching of the kingdom, goes to the Gentiles. The nations, "thought to be unclean by nature and filthy in their deeds," are the recipients of God's greatest gifts, the forgiveness

of sins and the Holy Spirit. We ought not to grow accustomed to how deeply scandalous the inclusion of the Gentiles is within the "Israel of God" (Gal 6:16) without, as Johnson notes, "requiring of them circumcision and the observance of Torah" (*PJPC*, 153).

37 Calvin, *Commentary on Acts*, 6:393.

38 Pelikan, *Commentary on Acts*, 132; Jennings, *Acts*, 131.

39 Davison, *Participation*, 32 (emphasis in original).

40 Davison, *Participation*, 116.

41 Davison, *Participation*, 127.

42 Davison, *Participation*, 120.

43 Where I think Davison's fine account is off the mark is in terms of how he emphasizes participation in "the Trinitarian Persons' own participation in one another." The "consummation of creaturely existence" that is "to participate in God" refers more to God's unicity than to, for example, our participation in the Father's begetting of the Son or of the Son's being begotten of the Father. Indeed, I do not know what that would mean. What I can say is that in heaven, creatures will experience what is common to the three in a way that completes and fulfills them in a manner utterly beyond what we may ask or imagine. See further Davison, *Participation*, 130.

44 Here I demur again from Sonderegger. She writes that "the God-world relation is not causal; rather it is unique." See Sonderegger, *Systematic Theology*, 2:75. I think it is causal (and therefore unique) because Scripture strongly intimates such a relation. Cornelius fears God because God causes him in such a way that Cornelius knows himself as created and upheld.

45 See further Sonderegger, *Systematic Theology*, 2:186.

46 Davison, *Participation*, 175.

47 Davison, *Participation*, 234.

48 Sonderegger, *Systematic Theology*, 2:278.

49 Calvin, *Commentary on Acts*, 7:73. Scripture's inspired character is not reckoned within Johnson's account. On the one hand, Johnson helpfully writes of "reading Luke and Acts as a single literary composition with coherence as a literary work and consistency in its religious outlook" (*PJPC*, 3). While I think that the language of "religious outlook" is quite thin

theologically, it is salutary to state that there is consistency. What is more important, however, is to ask what gives Luke-Acts the consistency that it does have. That consistency is there because of God. God speaks through Luke-Acts regarding the things God has done. Luke does not simply offer an "outlook" though that is in a sense true; more to the point, Acts offers us God. Put differently, God communicates with us through Acts, speaks through it as a literary and theological work, sanctifying it as it were, that we too might be related to God in faith and love. Here doctrine, specifically the doctrine of Scripture as inspired, "widens, rather than contracts, the realm of pious speculation and reverent imagination." David Bentley Hart, "Martin and Gallaher on Bulgakov," in *Theological Territories*, 58. The doctrine of inspiration widens the sense of "consistency," relating that to God, and offers a means of giving thanks to God as the one who anchors Scripture consistently in God's very self as one who wills to be known and loved as God.

50   Calvin, *Commentary on Acts*, 7:131. Acts 8:39 runs: "When they came up out of the water, the Spirit of the Lord snatched Philip away; the eunuch saw him no more, and went on his way rejoicing."

51   Kathryn Tanner, *God and Creation in Christian Theology: Tyranny or Empowerment?* (Minneapolis: Fortress, 2005), 71. When Tanner uses the language of "essential," her point is that God is not impacted by God's effects. God is not 'made' God in relation to them, for God has life in relationship to himself and not other things.

52   Tanner, *God and Creation*, 99.

53   Calvin, *Commentary on Acts*, 7:101.

54   Calvin, *Commentary on Acts*, 7:219.

55   See John 21:15–19.

56   Calvin, *Commentary on Acts*, 7:120.

57   Calvin, *Commentary on Acts*, 7:120.

58   Calvin, *Commentary on Acts*, 7:175.

59   I am at this juncture indebted to Paul J. Griffiths' *Christian Flesh* (Stanford, Calif.: Stanford University Press, 2018).

60 Tanner, *God and Creation*, 100.

61 Mascall, *Triune God*, 85, drawing from Aquinas, *ST* 2.2.23.3, ad2.

62 That said, I do not think Jesus will stand for all of us, for some of us will be saved by fire. See further 1 Cor 3:1–21, especially 15. Also compare 1 Cor 6:14: "And God raised the Lord and will also raise us by his power."

63 Calvin, *Commentary on Acts*, 6:150. The first part of the gospel is reconciliation "to God through Christ by the free imputation of righteousness."

64 Mascall, *Triune God*, 40.

65 Paul J. Griffiths, *Decreation: The Last Things of All Creatures* (Waco, Tex.: Baylor University Press, 2014), 48.

66 Griffiths, *Decreation*, 173.

67 Griffiths, *Decreation*, 216.

68 Griffiths, *Decreation*, 269. Where Johnson is quite insightful is in his description that the kingdom of Christ is both intensely personal and political. He notes that "Christians' conceptions of sin" are, unfortunately, "so concentrated on the weaknesses of the flesh" that "the willful and predatory practices of economic and political oppression of the weak" are overlooked. See *PJPC*, 95. Johnson reminds us that the personal and structural dimensions of sin are two sides of the same proverbial coin.

69 See further Griffiths, *Decreation*, 71.

70 See further Davison, *Participation*, 286.

71 Sonderegger, *Systematic Theology*, 2:359.

72 Sonderegger, *Systematic Theology*, 2:408, 401.

73 It is interesting, I think, that the first two volumes of Sonderegger's *Systematic Theology* follow broadly Thomas' architectonic in the *prima pars* of the *Summa Theologiae*, deploying Gilles Emery's principle of *redoublement* to elucidate that architectonic. See further Sonderegger, *Systematic Theology*, 2:210.

74 Sonderegger, *Systematic Theology*, 2:299.

75 For talk of God as "Event," see Sonderegger, *Systematic Theology*, vol. 2, for example pp. 234, 542.

76 Davison, *Participation*, 341.

77 This is Griffiths' locution (*Christian Flesh*, 50).

4 The Invocation of God

1   Calvin, *Commentary on Acts*, 6:19.

2   Interestingly, Barth notes that "the first feature of Calvin's concept of God is the thought of his divine sovereignty, which we also find, of course, in Luther, but not at any rate in the primary way in which it was at once for Calvin the basis of the relation between Lord and servant, the ethical relation between God and us." Karl Barth, *The Theology of John Calvin* (Grand Rapids: Eerdmans, 1995), 119.

3   Calvin, *Commentary on Acts*, 17:118.

4   The reader attuned to the conciliar Creeds will no doubt discern echoes here of the Son, who is life, and the Spirit, who is breath. Indeed, Paul's own mission to the Gentiles is seen here. What does God (the Father) give? He gives his only Son, and in giving him gives the Spirit.

5   Calvin, *Commentary on Acts*, 17:119.

6   Calvin, *Commentary on Acts*, 17:119.

7   Calvin, *Commentary on Acts*, 17:119. This Augustinian motif is wonderfully developed in Martin S. Laird, *An Ocean of Light: Contemplation, Transformation, and Liberation* (Oxford: Oxford University Press, 2019).

8   Calvin, *Commentary on Acts*, 17:119.

9   Calvin, *Commentary on Acts*, 17:119.

10   Calvin, *Commentary on Acts*, 17:119.

11   Calvin, *Commentary on Acts*, 17:119.

12   Tanner, *God and Creation*, 99.

13   Calvin, *Commentary on Acts*, 17:120.

14   Calvin, *Commentary on Acts*, 17:121.

15   Calvin, *Commentary on Acts*, 17:120.

16   Pelikan nicely discusses "the immensely complicated textual problems raised by this verse." See *Commentary on Acts*, 221–22.

17   Calvin, *Commentary on Acts*, 17:180.

18   Calvin, *Commentary on Acts*, 17:176.

19   Calvin, *Commentary on Acts*, 17:173.

20   Calvin, *Commentary on Acts*, 17:176.

21   See further Kucicki, *Acts*, 151.

22 See further Sonderegger's comments on realism in *Systematic Theology*, 2:201: "*Realism*, as I use it, refers to anything that is *there* and can make itself felt."

23 Sonderegger, *Systematic Theology*, 2:344.

24 Sonderegger, *Systematic Theology*, 2:380.

25 Sonderegger, *Systematic Theology*, 2:408.

26 See further Davison, *Participation*, 349, n. 2.

27 Sonderegger, *Systematic Theology*, 2:433.

28 Przywara, *Analogia Entis*, 373.

29 Davison, *Participation*, 375.

30 See further Davison, *Participation*, 357–65.

31 I am at something of a loss to describe the sharp contrast Calvin postulates between a strict education in accordance with "ancestral law" and the knowledge of God (Acts 22:3). This is especially so in light of Luke 24:27 wherein, "beginning with Moses and all the prophets, he [Jesus] interpreted to them the things about himself in all the scriptures." It is my understanding that the "ancestral law" yields knowledge of God, whose "true substance" is Christ himself. See Calvin, *Commentary on Acts*, 17:200. Christ abolishes the cultic dimension of the law, what Calvin calls "the outward use," though not the law's substance, which is Christ himself.

32 Here, too, it is appropriate to raise concerns about how God's encountering of Paul chastens Johnson's rather flat sense of what Acts is in favor of a more supernaturally charged description. In terms of what Acts is, I think Johnson's following description is puzzling, to say the least. Johnson describes it "not as a work of bland historiography but as a thrilling act of utopian imagination." I do not know that it means to think of it as an "act of utopian imagination" (*PJPC*, 5). If Johnson means by that that Luke's agency as a writer is drawn up into God's speech, then that is well and good enough. That said, the notion that Luke's "utopian imagination" is on display is dramatically reductionistic. What is present, instead, is apostolic proclamation, and how all things related to that. Accordingly, Acts is not so much "a normative prescription for how things ought to be" but a normative description for how things are: God raised Jesus—that is how things are. This

statement is both an indicative and imperative. It is a claim about the Father/Son (and Spirit) relationship—its immutability—and a command: repent, believe, and be baptized, witnessing in life and death to the forgiveness of sins.

33 Jennings, *Acts*, 176.
34 Calvin, *Commentary on Acts*, 17:219.
35 Calvin, *Commentary on Acts*, 17:221.
36 Calvin, *Commentary on Acts*, 17:220.
37 Calvin, *Commentary on Acts*, 17:217.
38 Calvin, *Commentary on Acts*, 17:279.
39 Calvin, *Commentary on Acts*, 17:252.
40 Calvin, *Commentary on Acts*, 17:250.
41 Calvin, *Commentary on Acts*, 17:278.
42 Calvin, *Commentary on Acts*, 17:251.
43 Calvin, *Commentary on Acts*, 17:308.

5 The Fear of God

1 Calvin, *Commentary on Acts*, 6:394. Note that I am working with Levering's definition of election as "the eternal plan of the historical missions of the Son and Spirit for building up the people of God." See *Predestination*, 34.
2 Calvin, *Commentary on Acts*, 7:119.
3 Calvin, *Commentary on Acts*, 7:121, 125.
4 Calvin, *Commentary on Acts*, 7:126.
5 Calvin, *Commentary on Acts*, 7:176.
6 Calvin, *Commentary on Acts*, 7:190.
7 Calvin, *Commentary on Acts*, 7:187.
8 Calvin, *Commentary on Acts*, 7:218.
9 Denys Turner, *God, Mystery, and Mystification* (Notre Dame, Ind.: University of Notre Dame Press, 2019), 24.
10 Turner, *God, Mystery, and Mystification*, 12.
11 Calvin, *Commentary on Acts*, 7:277.
12 Calvin, *Commentary on Acts*, 7:277.
13 Tanner, *God and Creation*, 79.
14 Turner, *God, Mystery, and Mystification*, 157.
15 Turner, *God, Mystery, and Mystification*, 145, 146.
16 Turner, *God, Mystery, and Mystification*, 163.

17 Mascall draws this insight from Bernard Lonergan. Eric L. Mascall, *Theology and the Gospel of Christ: An Essay in Reorientation*, 2nd ed. (London: SPCK, 1984), xx.

18 Turner, *God, Mystery, and Mystification*, 157.

19 See further Karl Barth's magisterial treatment of this theme in *CD* IV/1.

20 Mascall, *Theology and the Gospel of Christ*, 8.

21 Mascall, *Theology and the Gospel of Christ*, 1.

22 See further Tanner, *God and Creation*, 163.

23 Calvin, *Commentary on Acts*, 7:87.

24 Calvin, *Commentary on Acts*, 7:257.

25 Calvin, *Commentary on Acts*, 7:258.

26 Calvin, *Commentary on Acts*, 7:268.

27 Calvin, *Commentary on Acts*, 7:299.

28 Calvin, *Commentary on Acts*, 7:301. Johnson makes a helpful and insightful point about exorcisms and healings. He notes that they "find their term in the restoration of persons to community." (*PJPC*, 161) The salutary point is that restoration involves the vertical dimension—especially in the case of exorcisms. The vertical dimension assumes the horizontal, restoration to fellowship and communion with God (the vertical) and the neighbor (the horizontal).

29 Calvin, *Commentary on Acts*, 7:311.

30 See Sonderegger, *Systematic Theology*, 1:48.

31 Sonderegger, *Systematic Theology*, 1:106.

32 Sonderegger, *Systematic Theology*, 1:422.

33 Sonderegger, *Systematic Theology*, 1:173.

34 Thomas writes, "It is also clear that the divine will is God's willing itself. For I have shown that the will in God is the same as the good willed by him." See Thomas Aquinas, *Compendium of Theology*, trans. Richard J. Regan (Oxford: Oxford University Press, 2009), §34 (p. 34).

35 Aquinas, *Compendium*, §101 (p. 81).

36 Aquinas, *Compendium*, §101 (p. 81).

37 Sonderegger, *Systematic Theology*, 1:341.

38 Sonderegger, *Systematic Theology*, 1:81.

39 Sonderegger, *Systematic Theology*, 1:33.

40   Sonderegger, *Systematic Theology*, 1:312.

41   Sonderegger, *Systematic Theology*, 1:330.

42   Sonderegger, *Systematic Theology*, 1:338.

43   Sonderegger, *Systematic Theology*, 1:434.

44   Sonderegger, *Systematic Theology*, 2:277.

45   Williams, *Christ*, 220.

46   Williams, *Christ*, 246.

47   See for example Williams, *Christ*, 5.

48   Williams, *Christ*, 35.

49   Williams, *Christ*, 40.

50   Williams, *Christ*, 49.

51   Williams, *Christ*, 64.

52   Williams, *Christ*, 83.

53   See further Williams, *Christ*, 86.

54   Williams, *Christ*, 97.

55   While I would not for a moment dispute that "the church's common life" is witness, I would disagree with Johnson's sense that it "is its first and most important witness, its most public and persuasive form of politics" (*PJPC*, 184). My concern is that Johnson does not allow for the (largely) apostate character of much of the church's life and witness (as is the case with Israel). Yes, there are moments of transparency and lived intimacy between God and the church, the church as a robust witness to God's raising of Jesus, but even then, its politics, such as they are, have potency because of the promise of God to bear witness through his covenant people (as now inclusive of the Gentiles) "until the time of universal restoration" (Acts 3:21). I do not thereby discount the political character of the church's common life. That said, I do think it needs to be articulated in a way that is mindful of how the "overwhelming preponderance of Christian history has amounted to little more than a sustained apostasy from the apostolic nature of the church." See Hart, "Tradition and Authority," 117.

56   Williams, *Christ*, 101.

57   Aquinas, *ST* 3.7.8.

58   Aquinas, *ST* 3.5, ad1.

59   Aquinas, *ST* 3.7.2, ad1.

60   See Aquinas, *ST* 3.7.6.

61   Ambrose of Milan, *De Officiis*, trans. Ivor J. Davidson (Oxford: Oxford University Press, 2001), 145.

62   Ambrose, *De Officiis*, 139.

63   Metaphysical theism and open theism are incompatible with one another—thus my aversion to statements such as "God takes a great risk by pushing the community in this direction," that is, the direction of the Gentiles (*PJPC*, 157). God's purposes and their fulfillment are not risky to God. God's purposes are immutable precisely because God is. "There is no variation or shadow due to change" with God because God is the fullness and plenitude of being itself (Jas 1:17).

64   Aquinas, *ST* 3.7.6, ad3.

65   Dylan Schrader, "Christ's Fear of the Lord according to Thomas Aquinas," *Heythrop Journal* 62, no. 6 (2021): 1054.

66   Schrader, "Christ's Fear," 1054.

67   Mascall, *Theology and the Gospel of Christ*, 45.

6 Other Principal Points of Heavenly Teaching

1   Though this is said by Augustine of Scripture in general, it is more than appropriate to say it of the book of Acts in particular. See Augustine of Hippo, *Confessions* 3.5.9.

2   Calvin, *Commentary on Acts*, 6:57.

3   Calvin, *Commentary on Acts*, 6:60.

4   See Acts 7:42: "But God turned away from them and handed them over to worship the host of heaven, as it is written in the book of the prophets."

5   Aquinas, *ST* 3.53.1, ad2.

6   Aquinas, *ST* 3.53.1, ad3.

7   Aquinas, *ST* 3.53.1, ad2.

8   Aquinas, *ST* 3.53.4.

9   Aquinas, *ST* 3.53.4, ad1.

10   Aquinas, *ST* 3.53.4, ad3.

11   Aquinas, *ST* 3.53.4.

12   Augustine of Hippo, *In Joan. Evang* 94, cited in Aquinas, *ST* 3.57.1, ad3 (emphasis original).

13   Aquinas, *ST* 3.57.2, ad2.

14 Aquinas, *ST* 3.57.3, ad3.

15 Aquinas, *ST* 3.57.5.

16 Aquinas, *ST* 3.57.6.

17 Aquinas, *ST* 3.57.6.

18 Aquinas, *ST* 3.57.6, ad2.

19 Aquinas, *ST* 3.54.1.

20 Aquinas, *ST* 3.54.1, ad3.

21 Consider Acts 9:16: "I myself will show him how much he must suffer for the sake of my name."

22 Craig S. Keener, *Acts*, 4 vols. (Grand Rapids: Baker Academic, 2012–2015), 1:957.

23 Aquinas, *ST* 111.54.1, ad2.

24 Craig S. Keener, *Acts*, New Cambridge Bible Commentary (Cambridge: Cambridge University Press, 2020), 308.

25 Mascall, *Theology and the Gospel of Christ*, 10.

26 Aquinas, *ST* 3.55.3, ad1.

27 Aquinas, *ST* 3.55.5.

28 This is quite a different strategy than Paul's in his speeches to the Gentile audiences, focusing as he does on creation's testimony culminating in eschatological judgment.

29 Augustine of Hippo, *In Joan. Evang.* 121, on 20, 17, cited in Aquinas, *ST* 3.55.6, ad3.

30 Aquinas, *ST* 3.56.1, ad1.

31 Aquinas, *ST* 3.56.1, ad3.

32 Aquinas, *ST* 3.56.2, ad2.

33 Aquinas, *ST* 3.56.2, ad1. Thomas credits Augustine for this insight.

34 See Acts 10:42, Peter's speech to the Gentiles in Caesarea, wherein Peter states: "He commanded us to preach to the people and to testify that he is the one ordained by God as judge of the living and the dead."

35 The "of God" is present in many other parts of the Pauline corpus, for example, in 2 Cor 6:16, wherein Paul describes the believers as the "temple of God."

36 What is curious regarding Johnson's account is his assertion that the church continues the story of Jesus. See *PJPC*, 90. It is better to emphasize the agency of Jesus and the Spirit, first and foremost, and only then the church. The story of Jesus is the church's principle of intelligibility. The church does not continue the story.

Instead Jesus, through the Spirit, continues via the proclaimed word and sacrament to give rise to a people—the church—who sing his praises, and in singing to him the Father and the Spirit. The church inhabits Jesus' life, death, and resurrection, to be sure, but it does so as an earthen vessel to which he binds himself in obedience to the Father's will. Jesus is the agent of his presence in the world, clothed in the gospel, and all that because the Father raised him and will judge all in him.

37 Aquinas, *ST* 3.58.4, ad1.

38 Aquinas, *ST* 3.59.2, ad2.

39 Mascall, *Theology and the Gospel of Christ*, 144.

40 I concur with Johnson's sense that "the narrative from beginning to end is about what God has done." See *PJPC*, 16. But it is also about what God is doing, and what God continues to do, for God continues to fulfil the promise to forgive sins and judge all through his resurrected Son. God's activity is expressive of the fact that God is pure act, there being no potential in him. To speak primarily of what God has done underplays the sense in which God sustains things in accord with their end, that is, God himself.

41 Mascall, *Theology and the Gospel of Christ*, 211.

42 Mascall, *Theology and the Gospel of Christ*, 214, 221.

43 Mascall, *Theology and the Gospel of Christ*, 211.

44 Mascall, *Theology and the Gospel of Christ*, 212.

45 Mascall, *Theology and the Gospel of Christ*, 185.

46 Mascall, *Theology and the Gospel of Christ*, 146, 163.

47 Aquinas, *ST* 2.2.179.1, ad1.

48 Aquinas, *ST* 2.2.179.1.

49 Calvin, *Commentary on Acts*, 6:179.

50 Calvin, *Commentary on Acts*, 7:218.

51 Calvin, *Commentary on Acts*, 7:219.

52 Calvin, *Commentary on Acts*, 7:219.

53 Calvin, *Commentary on Acts*, 7:251.

54 Calvin, *Commentary on Acts*, 7:278.

55 Williams, *Christ*, 104–5.

56 Williams, *Christ*, 105 (emphasis added).

57 Williams, *Christ*, 114.

58 Williams, *Christ*, 165.

59 See Williams, *Christ*, 170.

60 See Williams, *Christ*, 170.
61 Williams, *Christ*, 217.
62 Williams, *Christ*, 236.
63 Williams, *Christ*, 240.
64 Williams, *Christ*, 248.
65 Williams, *Christ*, 247.
66 Williams, *Christ*, 249.
67 Williams, *Christ*, 263.
68 Williams, *Christ*, 269.
69 This is from the preface of the latest published volume of Webster's sermons. See John Webster, *Christ Our Salvation: Expositions and Proclamations*, ed. Daniel Bush (Bellingham, Wash.: Lexham, 2020), xvi.
70 See further the wide-ranging and thoughtful proposal of Simeon Zahl in *The Holy Spirit and Christian Experience* (Oxford: Oxford University Press, 2020).

Conclusion

1   Again, a doctrine of inspiration "widens," to use Hart's language, our sense of what is going on here. See Hart, "Martin and Gallaher on Bulgakov," 58. The issue is not so much whether "Luke's depiction of the church may or may not be based on facts from the past" as Luke's "depiction" attests the truth of the matters covered in Acts. Acts is neither "depiction" nor "construction" or for that matter "vision" pioneered as it were by Luke (*PJPC*, 7). Yes, the "inspiring spirit" is at work, but that is not enough (*PJPC*, 6). The Spirit is at work, yes, as God's gift poured out through his Son raising witnesses to the truth. The great gift— "the promise of the Father"—is for Gentiles too (Acts 1:4). What we have is not a spirit-grounded "imaginative construction" but apostolic witness to the truth (*PJPC*, 7). Luke is a witness to these things. A witness does not construct in a spirit-inspired way but receives, through the Spirit, eyes with which to see and ears with which to hear the truth and to respond accordingly.
2   Sonderegger, *Systematic Theology*, 2:240.

Bibliography

Ambrose of Milan. *De Officiis*. Translated by Ivor J. Davidson. Oxford: Oxford University Press, 2001.

Aquinas, Thomas. *Basic Writings of Saint Thomas Aquinas*. Edited by Anton C. Pegis. New York: Random House, 1945.

———. *Compendium of Theology*. Translated by Richard J. Regan. Oxford: Oxford University Press, 2009.

———. *Summa Theologiae*. Translated by Blackfriars. Cambridge: Cambridge University Press, 1964.

Augustine of Hippo. *Confessions*. Translated by Henry Chadwick. Oxford: Oxford University Press, 1991.

———. *The Trinity*. Translated by Edmund Hill. Brooklyn: New City Press, 1997.

Barth, Karl. *Church Dogmatics*. Edited by George W. Bromiley and Thomas F. Torrance. Edinburgh: T&T Clark, 1957–1969.

———. *The Theology of John Calvin*. Grand Rapids: Eerdmans, 1995.

Basil of Caesarea. *On the Holy Spirit*. Translated by Stephen Hildebrand. Yonkers, N.Y.: St. Vladimir's Seminary Press, 2011.

Boersma, Hans. *Seeing God: The Beatific Vision in Christian Tradition*. Grand Rapids: Eerdmans, 2018.

Calvin, Jean. *Calvin's New Testament Commentaries*. Vol. 6, *Acts 1–13*. Edited by David W. Torrance and Thomas F. Torrance. Grand Rapids: Eerdmans, 1994.

———. *Calvin's New Testament Commentaries.* Vol. 7, *Acts 14–28.* Edited by David W. Torrance and Thomas F. Torrance. Grand Rapids: Eerdmans, 1994.

———. *Institutes of the Christian Religion.* Translated by Ford Lewis Battles. Philadelphia: Westminster, 1960.

Church of England. *The Book of Common Prayer: 1662 Version (Includes Appendices from the 1549 Version and Other Commemorations).* London: David Campbell, 1999.

Crowe, Brendon. *The Hope of Israel: The Resurrection of Christ in the Acts of the Apostles.* Grand Rapids: Baker Academic, 2020.

Davison, Andrew. *Participation in God: A Study in Christian Doctrine and Metaphysics.* Cambridge: Cambridge University Press, 2019.

Fergusson, David. *The Providence of God: A Polyphonic Approach.* Cambridge: Cambridge University Press, 2019.

Gorman, Michael. *Aquinas on the Metaphysics of the Hypostatic Union.* Cambridge: Cambridge University Press, 2017.

Griffiths, Paul J. *Christian Flesh.* Stanford, Calif.: Stanford University Press, 2018.

———. *Decreation: The Last Things of All Creatures.* Waco, Tex.: Baylor University Press, 2014.

Hart, David Bentley. "Martin and Gallaher on Bulgakov." In Hart, *Theological Territories,* 55–64.

———. "Remarks Made to Jean-Luc Marion regarding Revelation and Givenness." In Hart, *Theological Territories,* 26–44.

———. "Should Science Think?" In Hart, *Theological Territories,* 150.

———. *Theological Territories: A David Bentley Hart Digest.* Notre Dame, Ind.: University of Notre Dame Press, 2020.

———. "Tradition and Authority: A Vaguely Gnostic Meditation." In Hart, *Theological Territories,* 98–120.

Holmes, Christopher R. J. "The Procession of the Spirit: Eternal Spiration." In *The Orthodox Doctrine of the Trinity: What's at Stake in Recent Debates.* Edited by Matthew Barrett. Downers Grove, Ill.: IVP Academic, 2022.

———. "What Does Calvin's Engagement with Acts Teach Us about God's Providence?" *Journal of Reformed Theology* 15 (2021): 208–24.

Jennings, Willie James. *Acts.* Louisville, Ky.: Westminster John Knox, 2017.

Jenson, Robert W. *Ezekiel.* Grand Rapids: Brazos, 2009.

Johnson, Luke Timothy. *Prophetic Jesus, Prophetic Church: The Challenge of Luke-Acts to Contemporary Christians.* Grand Rapids: Eerdmans, 2011.

Keener, Craig S. *Acts.* 4 vols. Grand Rapids: Baker Academic, 2012–2015.

———. *Acts.* New Cambridge Bible Commentary. Cambridge: Cambridge University Press, 2020.

Kucicki, Janusz. *The Function of the Speeches in the Acts of the Apostles: A Key to Interpretation of Luke's Use of Speeches in Acts.* Leiden: Brill, 2018.

Laird, Martin S. *An Ocean of Light: Contemplation, Transformation, and Liberation.* Oxford: Oxford University Press, 2019.

Levering, Matthew. *Predestination: Biblical and Theological Paths.* Oxford: Oxford University Press, 2011.

Mascall, Eric L. *Theology and the Gospel of Christ: An Essay in Reorientation.* 2nd ed. London: SPCK, 1984.

———. *The Triune God: An Ecumenical Study.* Allison Park, Penn.: Pickwick, 1986.

Moehn, Wilhelmus H. Th. "Calvin as Commentator on the Acts of the Apostles." In *Calvin and the Bible,* edited by Donald K. McKim, 199–223. Cambridge: Cambridge University Press, 2006.

O'Donovan, Oliver. *Ethics as Theology.* Vol. 1, *Self, World, and Time.* Grand Rapids: Eerdmans, 2013.

———. *Ethics as Theology.* Vol. 2, *Finding and Seeking.* Grand Rapids: Eerdmans, 2014.

———. *Ethics as Theology.* Vol. 3, *Entering into Rest.* Grand Rapids: Eerdmans, 2017.

O'Meara, Thomas F. "Grace as a Theological Structure in the 'Summa theologiae' of Thomas Aquinas." *Recherches de Théologie Ancienne et Médiévale* 55 (1988): 130–53.

Pelikan, Jaroslav. *Commentary on Acts.* Grand Rapids: Brazos, 2005.

Przywara, Erich. *Analogia Entis: Metaphysics; Original Structure and Universal Rhythm.* Grand Rapids: Eerdmans, 2014.

Schrader, Dylan. "Christ's Fear of the Lord according to Thomas Aquinas." *Heythrop Journal* 62, no. 6 (2021): 1052–64.

Sonderegger, Katherine. *Systematic Theology*. Vol. 1, *The Doctrine of God*. Minneapolis: Fortress, 2015.

———. *Systematic Theology*. Vol. 2, *The Doctrine of the Holy Trinity: Processions and Persons*. Minneapolis: Fortress, 2020.

Tanner, Kathryn. *God and Creation in Christian Theology: Tyranny or Empowerment?* Minneapolis: Fortress, 2005.

Turner, Denys. *God, Mystery, and Mystification*. Notre Dame, Ind.: University of Notre Dame Press, 2019.

Webster, John. *Christ Our Salvation: Expositions and Proclamations*. Edited by Daniel Bush. Bellingham, Wash.: Lexham, 2020.

———. "Mercy." In *God without Measure: Working Papers in Christian Theology*, vol. 2, *Virtue and Intellect*, 49–66. London: T&T Clark, 2015.

———. "Principles of Systematic Theology." In *The Domain of the Word: Scripture and Theological Reason*, 133–49. London: T&T Clark, 2012.

Wilcoxen, Matthew. *Divine Humility: God's Morally Perfect Being*. Waco, Tex.: Baylor University Press, 2019.

Williams, Rowan. *Christ the Heart of Creation*. London: Continuum, 2018.

Zahl, Simeon. *The Holy Spirit and Christian Experience*. Oxford: Oxford University Press, 2020.

Zwingli, Ulrich. *On Providence and Other Essays*. Translated by William John Hinke. Eugene, Oreg.: Wipf and Stock, 1999.

Index of Authors and Subjects

human nature, 26, 58
humanity: as ignorant, 18–19,
79–80, 154; as "Israelitish,"
26; as race, 15; Christ's, 34, 37,
42–43, 44–46; and divinity,
40–41
humility, 37, 50, 84, 117
hypostatic union: Christ's grace,
52; and Christ's resurrection,
126; and participation, 38; the
church, 141–42, 144–49; and
Thomas Aquinas, 40–42

idolatry, 87; and fear of God,
111–12
ignorance, 15, 79–80, 101, 137,
154, 155
immortality, believers': see Hope,
the Spirit's
invocation (prayer): and
creation, 76–83; and grace,
83–88; and repentance, 88–92;
and salvation, 96–97; and
testimony, 92–96
Israel: apostasy of, 14–16, 19,
58–59, 119, 121; and Gentiles,
57–58, 63; and grace, 51; Judas
as type of, 4; and judgment,
48; and new covenant, 56–57;
and Paul (apostle), 90–92;
repentance of, 17–19; salvation
of, 25–26

Jennings, Willie James, 55, 62,
90, 171n4, 172n31
Jenson, Robert W., 17–18, 63,
165n46
Jesus: see Christ
Jews: see Israel
Johnson, Luke Timothy, 161n20,
161–62n23, 162n1, 163n11,

164n23, 165n42, 167n1,
168–69n38, 170n77, 171n6,
172–73n36, 173n49, 175n68,
177–78n32, 179n28, 180n55,
182–83n36, 183n40
Judas: apostasy of, 14, 15, 59,
119, 138; betrayal of, 3–5
judgment, final: Christ as judge,
47–50, 94; foretold, 4; God as
judge, 20, 22, 93–94, 134; and
invocation, 81–83; and nature,
81

Keener, Craig S., 182n22, 182n24
kingdom, Christ's: as theocentric,
29; and faith, 144; and grace,
29–32; and the Holy Spirit, 128
knowledge of God, 105–6; see
also natural knowledge of God
Kucicki, Janusz, 161n20, 176n21

Laird, Martin S., 176n7
law of God: and ethics, 88; and
grace, 49–50, 63; purpose,
24–26
Levering, Matthew, 163n14,
163n15, 178n1
likenesses, to God: humanity as,
19, 20, 37; creatures as, 100,
112–14
listening exercise, vii, xiii
Lord's Supper: see Eucharist, the
love: see charity (virtue)

Mascall, Eric L., 172n24, 179n17;
on charity (virtue), 107; on
the church, 136, 139–40; on
the Holy Spirit, 54–55, 60; on
tradition, xii
mercy, God's: and creatures,
23; and expulsion of defects,

Index of Scripture and Ancient Sources

ANCIENT SOURCES